Creating Courses for Adults

Department of
Adult & Community Education

Creating Courses for Adults

DESIGN FOR LEARNING

Ralf St. Clair

A Wiley Brand

Published by Jossey-Bass
A Wiley Brand
One Montgomery Street, Suite 1000, San Francisco, CA 94104-4594—www.wiley.com, www.josseybass.com/highereducation

Jossey-Bass books and products are available through most bookstores. To contact Jossey-Bass directly call our Customer Care Department within the U.S. at 800-956-7739, outside the U.S. at 317-572-3986, or fax 317-572-4002.

Wiley publishes in a variety of print and electronic formats and by print-on-demand. Some material included with standard print versions of this book may not be included in e-books or in print-on-demand. If this book refers to media such as a CD or DVD that is not included in the version you purchased, you may download this material at http://booksupport.wiley.com. For more information about Wiley products, visit www.wiley.com.

Library of Congress Cataloging-in-Publication Data

Library of Congress Cataloging-in-Publication Data has been applied for and is on file with the Library of Congress.

ISBN 9781118438978 (paper); ISBN 9781118746905 (ebk.); ISBN 9781118747056 (ebk.)

Printed in the United States of America
FIRST EDITION

PB Printing   10 9 8 7 6 5 4 3 2 1

The Jossey-Bass Higher and
Adult Education Series

CONTENTS

PART ONE Core Factors in Teaching

ONE All About You   3

Contents

PREFACE

The big idea of this book is that education for adults has to be designed. Whether it's a one-hour class on wine tasting or a four-month language course, there are some key decisions that must be made as the course is crafted. One striking thing about teaching is that people tend to see it as easy—until they have to do it. This is not a mistake that we make about skydiving or baking a cake. I think that this often happens because people's favorite teachers have done a pretty good job and did not seem to struggle too much. By its very nature, good teaching conceals all the thinking, planning, and decision making that goes on behind the scenes in order to present participants with a seamless and natural-feeling process. This is impressive, but it's not very helpful when you are trying to do it yourself and provide a good educational experience to another person or group of people—then the behind-the-scenes action takes on a whole new importance and urgency. The purpose of this book is to open the curtain a little on the backstage work and provide insights into the way that good teachers of adults do what they do and, equally important, why.

This book is aimed at people who want to learn more about putting together courses for adults. If you are new to teaching, it'll take you through the key decisions you will need to make in planning and delivering your course. If you have a little experience, the book will give you an opportunity to reflect on your approach and come to some new perspectives. Educators make many decisions that seem natural but that have important implications for our teaching and learning practices, including how much people in our classes can actually learn. This book starts from the position that nobody is an intuitive or completely natural teacher and that all teachers have to make a series of choices as they put courses together. The decisions they make are important and far-reaching and deserve to be considered carefully.

For me, one of the most important aspirations is to be a responsible educator. This does not mean that you are serious all the time, or that you are a perfect teacher. It does mean, however, that you take the role of educator seriously and try to find ways to fulfill that role as well as you possibly can. It means thinking about what went well, or not so well, in your teaching and how you will respond to that. And it means starting off with a plan that is backed up with justification and good decision making. As educators we are responsible for the way a group of people feels about a topic or about themselves as learners, and we need to rise to that responsibility.

There's an old story about a man whose car breaks down in a small town in the mountains. He calls a mechanic, and a grizzled old guy turns up in dirty overalls with a cigarette hanging out of the side of his mouth. He looks at the car and says he can fix it for $300. The man, many miles from home, feels he has no choice, and agrees. The mechanic walks back to the truck, gets a big hammer, comes back to the car and hits the engine. The car starts immediately, and purrs like a kitten. "Hey!" says the man. "I'm not paying you $300 for hitting my engine with a hammer!" The mechanic replies, "No, you're not. You're paying $5 for the hit and $295 for knowing where to hit it!"

To me, this story seems like a good analogy for teaching. All too often we see the "hit" but not all the knowledge that goes into shaping it. And just like in the story, the true value of teaching is not the act of teaching but all the thought, preparation, and experience that lies behind it. This book sets out to give you a way to think through questions about where the hammer should be directed to get the car started. It may not give you $295 worth of knowledge right away, but I hope it will provide a starting point.

The use of design as the central idea of this book is a deliberate choice. We live in a world permeated with human design (if you look around at this moment, I'd be surprised if you can see one object that is not designed), but we do not think about it too much. Even the simplest objects, such as a sheet of paper, have been deliberately designed to look as they do. What size should it be? How dense? How thick? Should it have lines? Should it have added clay to make it shiny? Should there be recycled content? If we want to think about the world around us, it seems to me that a key step is recognizing the degree to which things are designed and the decisions that have to be made during that process. The same applies to teaching. The many decisions that have to be made during course planning and delivery can seem overwhelming, and thinking about it as a problem of design can help to get the issues under control and impose some kind of organization.

For simplicity, I have written this book as if there will be one educator and a group of learners, as this is probably the most common arrangement in the teaching of adults. The same sorts of questions and concerns will apply in situations where there is one educator and one learner, or several of each. The key to design is the relationship between the folks with the responsibility to organize learning and those who come to learn, and the nature of this relationship need not fundamentally change because there are more or less of each.

The design of this book itself can be summarized in a nine-cell framework (see Figure 1). The central three boxes are the core factors that have to be taken into account when creating courses. *Educator* factors are the things that you as teacher bring to the teaching and learning process, such as your experience and preferences. *Learner* factors are the influences that your students bring to the situation, including their biographies and their expectations for the class. *Context* factors are

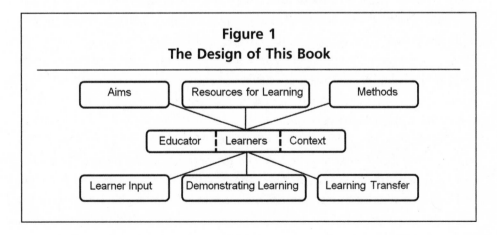

Figure 1
The Design of This Book

| Aims | Resources for Learning | Methods |

| Educator | Learners | Context |

| Learner Input | Demonstrating Learning | Learning Transfer |

the way the actual location of the class affects things, including whether you are working in an educational setting or a corporate setting where teaching is not the main business. The type of subject you are teaching also enters into these factors.

These factors are then discussed in terms of six groups of decisions you have to make about your educational work, with a chapter for each. For example, *demonstrating learning* can be approached through what you as instructor value, what learners enjoy, or what the context demands. In most situations, there will be some kind of balance among the three. The sections within the chapters talk about the sorts of questions you need to think through in order to make an informed and thoughtful decision about that area. This book does not argue for any particular approach—say, that multiple choice tests are better than pop quizzes—rather, I wish to make you aware of a range of options and some of the positive and negative effects of each.

In the final chapter I present the framework as whole, summarizing the key decisions in each area. This is not intended to replace the rest of the discussion, but will hopefully be useful as a design tool. In Appendix A there is a blank copy of the framework with room for your own notes and comments.

At this point you may be wondering if having a list of decisions to make will actually help you to make those decisions. Might it be better to have a list of techniques and approaches that could be applied where necessary? I believe that a list of techniques would be less helpful than it might appear at first because teaching is an intensely personal activity, and you have to find the fit that is right for you if you want to come across as credible and be effective. Any educators who want to build their practice must create their programs around a set of key questions (Sork, 2000). Thinking back on my own start as an educator of adults more than twenty years ago, it would have been most valuable to have an outline of decisions I would need to take and a few options for each. I certainly did not want to be told what to do, a whole lot of theory, or even how to do it—my interest was in understanding the process and building my own competence. I hope this book can assist with that process.

Before looking at design in a little more detail, however, I would like to comment on the idea of power that runs through this book. By power I mean, put simply, the ability to get things done the way you think they should be done. Whether we like it or not (usually not), power permeates the work we do as educators (Cervero & Wilson, 1994), and it would be naïve to think that educators make design decisions in a completely open context. In education power can be at the level of our societies, which often decide who gets access to high-quality education and who does not, as well as which knowledge is worth learning. It can also appear at much more local levels, concerning how much say the educator or the learners have in the class process. Negotiation, as discussed in Chapter Three, is a particularly important strategy if there is a disagreement between the educator and the people who have the power to decide the way things should be done.

At the same time, it is also useful to know where the power lies even if there are never any conflicts. It seems reasonable that committed educators would want to understand who or what was influencing their work, and who would have to be involved if any changes were to be made. Power is discussed in this book not because of any assumption that all educators are going to be involved in radical change processes, but because knowing who controls the context is essential professional knowledge.

It is important to add that this book does not set out to cover *all* the knowledge that we have regarding teaching and training adults. There are decades of studies on these issues, many of them of really high quality. This book should be regarded as only a starting point for people who want to go deeply into this literature. In this volume the priority has been to provide the information you need immediately to get started, or to enrich your practice if you have already taken the first steps.

WHY DESIGN?

The central idea of this book is that education for adults should be designed carefully and well. The immediate question is, of course, what counts as good design. People often think of design as being about the way something looks—for example, an icon on an iPhone or even the phone itself. There is no doubt that aesthetic appeal is an important part of good design, but it is only a part. A design that stands out as excellent fuses visual attractiveness with a well-thought-through use of materials and attention to function. This does not mean that design has to be fancy. As Antoine de Saint-Exupéry said, "Perfection is achieved, not when there is nothing more to add, but when there is nothing left to take away."

In many cases the best-designed artifacts look the most straightforward, but that doesn't happen by accident. Currently Apple products are seen as the epitome of good design. Anybody who has seen a toddler play with an iPad can understand why. It's a computer thousands of times more powerful than those that took the Apollo flights to the moon, but a three-year old can make it work. That is an astonishing victory of design over complexity.

When humans design things, whether objects or plans of action, they are exercising deliberate choices. That choice may be to go along with existing ways of doing things, but that's still default by design. If we choose to make changes, this can be thought of as devising "courses of action aimed at changing existing situations into preferred ones . . . Design, so construed, is the core of all professional training; it is the principal mark that distinguishes the professions from the sciences" (Simon, 1981, p. 129). For us as educators, design of teaching and learning is the center of our profession.

My own favorite school of design originated in Weimar Germany: the Bauhaus. Their interest was in taking the new materials of the time and making beautifully simple objects. The ability to make curves in tubular steel and bend plywood to match those curves, for example, led to furniture that looks amazingly organic but can be mass-produced. Bauhaus saw art and industry not as contradictory, but as consistent and mutually supportive.

One of the modern inheritors of the Bauhaus approach is designer Dieter Rams, who has become world-famous designing industrial objects for Braun and furniture for Vitsoe. Interestingly, he is cited as an influence by the designer of the Apple iPhone and iPad. Rams is seen as a master of design, and he has won a great number of awards for his work. In the 1980s he formulated a set of ten principles for good design (San Francisco Museum of Modern Art, 2011), to which I have added brief notes on the ways that I see them applying to education. Good design:

1. Is innovative—Educators work in constantly changing contexts, and the ways that we respond need to change accordingly. Although notes from the course I taught last year can be a useful framework for this year's course, I still need to recognize the characteristics of a different group of learners, and my own thinking will have moved on as well. In addition, there are always new resources to draw upon. Innovation, in this case, does not have to mean dramatic reinvention; often simply being open to new ideas and new approaches is what is needed.

2. Makes a product useful—Good design does not get in the way of teaching. Suppose, for example, that you are in week three of a course and somebody asks a question on material that will not be covered until week five. What do you do? You can either stick to your design or go with the flow of the learners. I'd say that it is always better to use the teachable moment, and the design of your class should allow for a degree of looseness to maximize its usefulness to participants.

3. Is aesthetic—I have always been struck by the extent to which the aesthetics of education matter. This means everything from the most simple—high-quality handouts that are attractive to read—to the most complex—an attractive place for people to meet and discuss what they are learning. Not paying attention to these seemingly trivial aspects of the work can disrupt learning very quickly.

4. Makes a product understandable—In other words, students need to understand the format of the course, where it is going, and how they can be successful in the course. The materials and the instructor need to communicate explicitly about the intention of the course and the route that will be taken to get there. Mystification does not create confidence!

5. Is unobtrusive—The design of an educational program should be thought of like a tool, increasing the "usability" of the course by the learners. Anything that makes the course harder to understand or to move through should have a clear educational rationale or be removed. It took me a long time to learn to "de-fancify" my teaching!

6. Is honest—It's important to let learners know what they can and cannot expect from the course. There is nothing to be gained from overpromising. Expectations should be clear and realistic, and all aspects of the course should support them.

7. Is long-lasting—Even though innovation is desirable, it's worth taking the time to ensure that the principles you have used to design the course are going to be around for a while. Think through what's going to matter about the course or program in three years, or five years. It's not the details but rather the overall experience that can be developed to be durable.

8. Is thorough down to the last detail—Thinking things through can be a mark of respect toward learners. But it's also important to allow space for the learners to influence the shape of their own learning. Courses, as I will suggest later in this book, are really cocreations of the instructor and the learners. There is an important difference, however, between open design and a design that's full of holes!

9. Is environmentally friendly—This may seem like a strange principle to include in the discussion of the design of education. This principle is becoming more and more important in education, however, in a range of ways. There is a literal meaning that suggests being careful about resources, even down to the detail of not using too much photocopying. There's also a more metaphorical application, which reflects the need to ensure that the educational experience fits with the environment. This is explored in more detail in Chapter Three.

10. Is as little design as possible. One mistake designers make is to do too much—to give the car a shiny chrome grill, a rear wing, and enormous fins. In the same way, educators can try to pack too much, and too much variety, into their teaching. This is exhausting for everybody involved, and it limits the opportunities for students to shape their own learning. A program with a few good activities and time to talk about them is almost always better than a whole heap of less-focused components.

This may seem like a lot of things to think about, but it's not necessary to think about them all every time you make a decision regarding your teaching. They fit together as a set of values or principles that can guide your development work. The rest of this book will discuss an approach that reflects these ideas, pulling them together so that they don't always have to be explicitly considered.

When thinking about putting together a course or a class, one lesson from design is perhaps the most important: the idea that design is never really finished. It is not possible to make something perfect and then stop. One of the most famous expressions of this notion comes from Apple Computer, who summarizes the design process as "Express, Test, Cycle" (Edson, 2013, p. 113). This means that they try something, see how it goes, and then, based on that knowledge, try something else. Educators often find this difficult, believing they have to be perfect every time, and of course there are good reasons why we want to work with learners as effectively as possible. But we need to invest time and thought in being effective, and we also need to be willing to experiment with different approaches.

The idea of design provides educators with some frameworks for thinking about their work, as well as a way to distance themselves from their educational decision making a tiny bit. Our teaching will always be close to us, in the sense that our approach is profoundly shaped by who we are, but it is incredibly valuable to have the space to reflect on our teaching and play with the structure a little. One hallmark of responsible and effective educators is that they find ways to frame their practice explicitly. By this I mean that they don't just go and "teach"; they have a plan with a rationale and resources to support that plan. This both gives their teaching some shape and makes it easier to think about possible adjustments.

PERSPECTIVE ON LEARNING

The general theoretical framework of this book is sociocultural learning theory, a way of looking at learning that underlines the social processes involved. Whereas other theories are more interested in what happens in the brains of learners or in the effective transmission of ideas from instructors to learners, sociocultural models are based on an interest in what happens between people in teaching and learning situations. This approach (which will be discussed more fully in Chapter Three) shapes what I believe good teaching looks like at a fundamental level. Based on a number of research articles examining sociocultural theories in practice (see, for example, King, 2012) it is possible to define four key values of good teaching. Throughout this book I will be applying these values as the hallmarks of effective teaching, as I do within my own work as an educator. Teaching should:

- Encourage active learning. People need to learn by *doing* wherever possible, rather than simply hearing or reading about how to do.
- Allow people to have some control over their own learning.
- Build connections between what is being learned and the experiences of learners, moving over time toward more complex ideas.
- Encourage collaboration and conversation between learners. One of the great insights of sociocultural theory is that people learn more powerfully together than they do individually.

These values can be applied in almost every teaching and learning context, which means that the same kinds of design questions, albeit in different forms, arise in each situation. In this book, for example, I have not drawn a clear line between face-to-face and online learning, because the same sorts of questions need to be addressed in both cases. The answers may well differ, but the ways educators approach the questions should be very similar.

FURTHER INFORMATION

In Appendix B (the last section of this book) I have provided some suggestions for places to go to find further information on the topics discussed here. It is not a list of specific resources, which would be incredibly difficult to keep updated and relevant and even then would not necessarily fit with individuals' interests. Instead, it is a brief list of starting points, any one of which can help you find what you need to know. I hope you find it helpful.

ACKNOWLEDGMENTS

Tom started my interest in this area many years ago, and Dan helped deepen it.

I'd like to thank McGill University and my colleagues there for putting up with my mysterious absences. I'm not sure everybody believed I was "working on my book." Special acknowledgment to my friend Lise for the scones (and general brilliance) and to Mike for being solid and fun, sometimes simultaneously.

David Brightman, the editor at Wiley, made it all happen after years of thinking about it. His support was constant and wonderful. Imagine, an editor who trusts the author! All remaining mistakes, misstatements, and confusions in the book are the fault of neither of us. We blame the Martians.

As always, this work is dedicated to Sylvie and the boys: Grant, Nicolas, and Joseph. Thank you.

ABOUT THE AUTHOR

Ralf St. Clair is a professor at the University of Victoria in British Columbia, Canada. He has been working in adult education for over thirty years as a practitioner, researcher, and consultant. Ralf grew up in Scotland, and his first qualifications were in community education from Moray House College in Edinburgh. He retains a concern about the ways in which education can support community and social movements, and still strongly believes in the link between education and social justice.

Ralf's PhD, completed at the University of British Columbia in 2000, was a study of how educators in a union literacy program create their curriculum. His research interests include literacy, the sociology of education, and First Nations education, as well as the ways young people form their ambitions for their adult lives. Ralf has worked in the United Kingdom, the United States, Canada, and several European countries, and continues to find adult education fascinating and challenging.

Ralf tries to ride his bike to work every day, even when it rains, and benefits from the intellectual and emotional support of a plump orange cat. His long-term aim is to restore a tractor for the local agricultural museum, which is a nice change from writing and research.

Creating Courses for Adults

Core Factors in Teaching

All About You

It has always seemed right to me to think of teaching as a craft. For any craft, one of the most important aspects is having the right tools and knowing how to use them to their best advantage. As a simple example, having high-quality masking tape makes it far easier to paint a house, but you need to know that it must be removed before the paint is completely dry if you don't want to leave marks (and bits of tape stuck to your walls). One of the differences between teaching and other crafts is that the main tools are the educators themselves. When you are teaching, your personality, your approach, and your values influence the form and outcomes of the process. This is such an important aspect of teaching that it makes a huge difference to be aware of who you are as a teacher and how those strengths may play out in the classroom.

This chapter lays out the importance of the educator's experience and philosophy in shaping the educational process, and leads readers through some options for knowing more about who they are as educators.

By the end of this chapter you will

- Understand the importance of who you are to the way you teach
- Know why reflection on your practice matters
- Have some ideas about how to use your experience

WHY WHO YOU ARE AND WHAT YOU'VE DONE MATTERS

When somebody walks into a room to start instruction, he brings his history with him. On the factory floor, the senior employee asked to train new employees has received training in the past and also has experience of working in the factory. The football coach talking to the team is drawing on knowledge and experience of coaching as well as a great deal of time watching games and usually playing as well. The charge nurse orientating new nurses to ward procedures is drawing on work experience, standard procedures, and the way she herself was trained when she arrived. In each case, the educator has a huge range of experiences as well as many hours of formal and informal learning to draw upon.

These background factors can make a big difference to the ways people teach. The overall approach people bring to teaching includes their actions, their beliefs, and their intentions (Pratt, 2002). Actions are observable, and it intuitively makes sense that they demonstrate the approach of the teacher, but beliefs and intentions may not be so obvious. Beliefs, in this context, are the assumptions the individual makes about the purposes and processes of education, and intentions are the outcomes the educator hopes for. Many educators assume that participants learn only from their actions, because these actions represent deliberate communication. Learners do more than this: they learn from the whole context, and that context is shaped by beliefs and intentions. This can be illustrated by thinking about a trades class where the instructor is strongly anti-union. In this case the students learn about installing drywall, but the instructor will choose examples and frame teaching in a way that does not acknowledge the unionized reality of most of the students' working lives. Even if nothing explicit is ever said, the students will pick up on the lack of references and most likely get the message.

One influential factor is the educator's own educational experience. Somebody who did well at school when she was young, tended to be friendly with teachers, and enjoyed reading and writing will have a particular view of teaching and learning. An educator who disliked school, was uncomfortable with the authority of teachers, and hated sitting still at a desk will have a very different perspective. These differing views make a huge difference to the sort of teaching these educators design and deliver, from the objectives through the process to the ways that learning is assessed. We could imagine that the first educator would be quite happy with a student essay as an assessment method, whereas the second would find marking essays excruciating and enjoy something "hands-on" a great deal more.

Ed Taylor (2003) conducted a very interesting study to understand more about the ways in which individuals' experiences in school affected their approach to educating adults. He talked to a number of aspiring adult educators about their experiences as school students and about their approach to being educators themselves. His results were striking, and they underscore the extent to which experience influences educators' practices.

Taylor found that when people are asked to talk about the most positive experiences they have had with teachers and to describe the ideal teacher, the similarities are very strong. So if a person has related well to a teacher who was friendly and supportive, then they describe the ideal teacher as a supportive person. Perhaps more surprising, they also describe themselves as friendly and supportive. The influence of positive experiences with schoolteachers seems to be very strong, even when the educator is thinking about teaching adults in a very different setting.

Previous learning experiences seemed to matter a lot as well, and they shaped how the educators in the study thought about learning. If an educator gained a great deal of insight through project-based learning, then she tended to use projects in her own teaching. It seems that if somebody is involved in an educational experience that suits her and helps her to learn, then she will try to recreate it in her own teaching. With regard to learning, one useful insight is that when asked about positive learning experiences, study participants tended to describe occasions when the teachers made learning engaging and interesting. These educators associated good teaching with effective transmission of existing knowledge rather than a more participatory or ground-up approach.

There are two important lessons from this study. First, teachers have a strong tendency to adopt a teaching style that they would enjoy if they were students, including the sort of techniques and classroom exercises chosen. It is not necessarily a problem that teachers teach as they wish to be taught. In many cases this will be a powerful approach, as the educators will bring insight and enthusiasm to the process. But I do believe that it is important for educators to know that they are doing this and to be aware of the preferences they are bringing to their teaching. For example, I like ideas very much and find them energizing, and this works pretty well with graduate students who love to discuss theory. But I also work with practitioners, who are busy people with a lot on their minds. For them, ideas are often interesting only if they are concretely linked to the complexities of their everyday experience, and it is important to respect this.

Knowing my preferences allows me to act thoughtfully and change my approach if another way of working might produce a better outcome for all involved.

The second insight from the study is the way people tend to think of good teachers as good transmitters of information, which reflects only one possible view of the way teaching and learning fit together. In the view of teaching adopted by Taylor's participants, only one side of the equation is considered—that of teaching—and learning is assumed to occur if teaching happens in the right way. Later in this chapter I will be describing other ways of thinking about these factors. Good teaching is not necessarily about transmitting a predetermined set of information in an efficient way—more often than not it is about management of a set of relationships, which may result in efficient transmission but ideally leads to a deeper exchange between the people involved.

The field in which the educator was trained can also be an influential factor (Jarvis-Selinger, Collins, & Pratt, 2007). For example, if you are a trained scientist your teaching might be very orientated toward facts, whereas somebody with a background in literature may want to encourage students to explore ideas and make arguments. Admittedly, this is a bit stereotypical, but it represents the way that different educational experiences can affect the educators' views of the types of knowledge that are most useful. The important thing is being aware of the extent to which your approach as an educator is influenced by this factor and how it is more or less helpful in different situations.

Length of experience in the classroom makes a big difference in teaching—in two different ways. On the positive side, research shows that schoolteachers with experience can be more effective teachers (Murnane & Phillips, 1981). In fact, the difference they discovered was very significant. Children taught by a teacher with five years of experience progressed four to five months more in a single year than those taught by one who was just beginning to teach. On the less positive side, one classic study suggests that over time teachers in schools become less concerned with building rapport with students and more focused on a "tight" process with clear expectations and rules (Rabinowitz & Rosenbaum, 1960). Even though this research looks at schoolteachers, it alerts us to the danger of becoming too rigid in our approach to teaching wherever we work.

These studies suggest that we have to think about our experience in order to ensure that we are making it work for us in positive ways. We need to find ways to hold onto the interest and enthusiasm with which educators start their career of teaching adults, and this chapter will give you tools that will allow you to do this. Before turning to this, though, I need to make one more point. As you go through the questions for reflection and the different philosophies in the next two sections, it is very likely that you will think "Well, it depends," or "With this group I would do that, with the other group something else," or "It changes with the aims of the class." These are absolutely fair reactions—teaching is a dynamic process, and it would be misleading to suggest that any educator approaches it in the same way every time. However, trying to understand your own favored approach can alert you to two aspects of your practice. The first is the starting points you tend to use. What do you take as the default position for teaching, the home base from which you work? The second is the gaps in your practice, the areas where you could potentially do more. Nobody is a perfect educator able to respond in an ideal way to every situation, but being aware of the less developed areas in your practice can be extremely helpful. The next sections look at some ways you can build deeper knowledge of these aspects of your teaching—a necessary step in mastering the tools of your trade.

REFLECTING ON YOUR APPROACH

It is quite useful to educators to understand their own perspective and how it grows out of their experience and any training they may have had. The process of understanding who you are as an educator, and of constantly thinking about how to improve your practice, is called *reflection*. Somebody who approaches his work in this way is called a *reflective educator*. This approach has many benefits—not only does it lead to better teaching, but reflective educators often find their work more interesting and challenging.

One person who has thought and written a lot about teaching adults is Stephen Brookfield (1995). He really pays attention to his own teaching practice and why he does the things he does, and he encourages others to do the same. For Brookfield, one of the keys to reflective teaching is identifying assumptions and questioning them.

For some educators, the assumptions that need to be identified might include that adults like to be told what to learn and how to learn it. These educators may believe that adults are busy and don't have time to work this out for themselves. For other educators, the key assumption might be that adults should always be included in course planning, as they are the experts on their own learning. For Brookfield the problem is not that one of these assumptions is wrong and the other right—it's that both represent absolute, unquestioned perspectives on teaching and learning.

Brookfield does not expect educators to adopt a completely open, relativistic approach. What he hopes is that teachers of adults will think about these things and how they play out in their particular teaching context. There are few final answers; really, all we have is a set of well-thought-through responses to a specific situation and set of learners.

On one hand, this is a really high standard to set. The expectation that teachers will genuinely reconsider their most basic beliefs on a continuing basis seems impossible to live up to! On the other hand, the call for an open attitude whereby we really think through what we are doing—and why—sounds like a practical and sensible idea. For many of us, who have a range of tasks other than teaching to deal with, this can be an important and attainable starting point.

The first question is how to begin this process. We get used to our own way of seeing the world, and it becomes transparent to us, like looking through a window. The trick is finding a way to make the glass visible. Sometimes educators get a feeling as they teach that something they are doing is not quite right and could be improved. Sometimes external factors have an influence on how educators think about things. Perhaps most often, educators find themselves thinking about things differently without really knowing why. In any of these situations, reflecting on our work can help us to understand what is happening.

As an example from my own practice, I used to dislike "learning outcomes" or "learning objectives" in my own teaching. They seemed to make education sound mechanical and reduce the opportunities for learners to shape the process and direction of the class. After many years, I started to see that having clear, well-defined objectives could go a long way in helping learners to plan their learning on an informed basis and make it easier for them to know what to expect. They can also provide a way for learners to call instructors to account, in that learning objectives can be seen as a contract between the participants. From this perspective, learning objectives do not limit the power of learners but contribute to that power on a number of levels. My understanding of this complexity came when I stepped back and really thought about something I had noticed—students I worked with often really liked objectives and would ask for them.

If they were not available, it could be really stressful for the students and immobilize them. I was struck by the fact that even if the objective was simply to "define the learning objective," that seemed to be valuable and useful for folk. At this point I began to realize the critical importance of the difference between *structure* and *constraint*. Students expect you, as the educator, to (1) help structure what from their experience can seem like a vast field of the unknown, and (2) not limit the ways in which they can cross it. Providing a few landmarks and warnings about the boggy areas is not the same thing as making them walk along a single previously mapped trail.

What helped me to understand this process was starting to write about it. I had become interested in quality systems in education, which require clear objectives before the educational process starts so that final outcomes can be measured. As I began to think through the implications, it became clear to me that I had been too simplistic in my approach.

Not everybody will reflect in this way, of course. Many educators prefer an informal journal in which they can write down important events and ideas. Sometimes people who write journals never go back and read them, having found that the process of writing was enough. Other educators do not like to write so much, but keep index cards (either literally or electronically) with details of things they've tried and what happened. Some experienced educators do not write anything at all but say that they reflect either through talking with colleagues or thinking over their classes. There is an important balance to be found here. On one hand, I do believe that it is important to find a way to structure reflection on your work as an educator—in fact, this can be considered in many ways as the mark of a professional in any field. On the other hand, it is also critical not to end up in the situation where reflection is a separate activity from teaching. This will not only reduce its effectiveness but also make it much harder to sustain.

Two ideas have shaped my thinking on reflection very strongly. The first is Donald Schön's (1983) work on reflection in action. Schön looked at a wide range of professionals, such as doctors and architects, and came to the conclusion that they were deeply reflective about their everyday practices, but this reflection was embedded in the actions they took as part of their work. There was not so much a separate activity called "reflection" as a conscious application of ideas to problem-solving. The practice and reflection upon it were inseparable. The second idea is the Buddhist concept of mindfulness, which (expressed very simply) refers to being conscious and thoughtful about what you are doing. Even if you are teaching a lesson for what seems like the millionth time, mindfulness asks you to be aware of what you are doing and why.

I think there is great value in educators' reflecting on their work and processing their experience—and this requires finding the approach that really works for them. It is not possible to tell somebody else what that approach is going to be. Some people will record copious detailed observations of their teaching, others jot a few notes, write a blog, or take a photo. "Questions for Reflection" can help you get started with your reflections, no matter how you choose to address them.

QUESTIONS FOR REFLECTION

- Who was your favorite teacher at school? What was it about this teacher that you liked? Was it teaching, personality, or both? In what ways does your teaching reflect these same values?

- Who was your least favorite teacher? Why? In what ways does your teaching avoid these same issues?

- Have you had a mentor in your life? What was important about this person's influence? Why did you respond to this mentor as you did?

- What do you dread about teaching? What seems difficult and ineffective?

- What do you love about teaching?

- In what situations do you feel most successful as a teacher?

- In what situations do you feel most challenged?

- How do you approach discipline in your classroom? Do you use humor in a way you are comfortable with?

- How prepared do you like to be when you enter a classroom? Do you think that coming into a class "empty-handed" disrespects the students or respects their contributions?

- If you could change one thing in your teaching, what would it be?

As you develop your own approach to reflections, there are a few criteria it can be helpful to bear in mind. Whatever your approach, it seems to me that reflections are most useful if:

- You can return to them at a later date.
- They are focused on a concrete problem or question—including the solution!
- They are based on an understanding of your teaching approach.

One way to inform and challenge your reflections is to understand a little more about how you think about teaching—which can all too easily be invisible. In the next section, I will lay out a few ideas for making your thinking more visible.

WHAT ARE WE DOING IT FOR?

One aspect of who we are as educators is how we think about education. What's the purpose of education generally, at the "big picture" level? What are we trying to achieve in our own classes? What matters most in the educational process? What ways of doing things will we support or not support?

There have been a number of attempts to bring the answers together and create a consistent way to frame the actions of educators in terms of their educational philosophy. Perhaps not surprisingly, this has been both challenging and not always entirely successful. In my many years of preparing adults to teach adults, this has always been the most complicated thing to discuss with my students, and the topic has not always really engaged people. Some have commented that the "philosophical" frameworks can seem artificial, too removed from real life, and oversimplified. I do have some sympathy with these concerns. After all, when you are struggling with establishing yourself as an educator, it does not really help to be told that Plato had the same difficulty. On balance, however, I believe strongly that some knowledge of these frameworks can provide insights into what you are hoping to achieve and, perhaps equally important, what sort of assumptions you wish to avoid.

To show how philosophy matters, consider the situation in which an educator has to prepare people for a written test such as the European Driving License, even though the students have not had much formal education and dislike "examinations." In this situation, there are various options open to the educator. One is finding an alternative way to measure their skills in a way that does not punish them for their past experiences. Another is working to strengthen their ability to complete a written test, such that their past experience need not prevent them from meeting the same standards as everybody else. The difference between these two options is philosophical, reflecting the educator's beliefs about assessment, about equity, and about the most respectful way to work with students with a limited educational background.

If you are interested in exploring your educational philosophy, there are two quite different ways to begin.

What Is Education For?

First, you can start with the overall and much broader question about what education, as a set of activities, is for. As you try to clarify your beliefs, different philosophies of education can provide a lot of food for thought. The most influential approach is probably that taken by John Elias and Sharan Merriam (1995), which identifies six different philosophical viewpoints that underpin adult education. The five related to practice are:

• *Liberal:* Interested in making sure that as many people as possible get access to the best of human ideas. The role of the educator is to ensure that learners have an opportunity to engage with and master this knowledge; the educator may also take on the role of expert.

• *Progressive:* Supports alternative ways of learning, such as problem-based learning and group learning. Educators working on this basis tend to take on a more facilitative role and to believe that knowledge comes out of exchanging ideas and experiences.

• *Behaviorist:* Focused on observable behavior and making changes in it. The role of the educator is to bring about and measure changes in behavior, often placing more weight on designing an environment that rewards the desired behaviors.

• *Humanist:* Chiefly concerned with the development of the person, with great importance placed on respecting and supporting people involved in education. The role of the educator is to facilitate development and growth in an appropriate manner.

• *Radical:* Interested in education as a means to support social change, justified by the inequities in current social structures. The role of the educator is to raise consciousness of unfair situations and help learners develop responses likely to bring about change.

These perspectives have generally been recognized as the main philosophical approaches for the last thirty years. Lorraine Zinn (1983) took these ideas in the early 1980s and created a tool that would allow educators to answer a number of questions and see where their beliefs best fit. In recent years this has been developed into an online tool that can be easily and quickly completed. This is an interesting exercise, especially when it suggests that you are not in the category you expected, and I recommend that everybody, whether an experienced educator or not, give it a go.

One insight that comes from looking at the philosophy of teaching adults is that the dominant perspectives have changed significantly over time. For example, the GI Bill in the United States, and similar measures elsewhere, were strongly rooted in liberal traditions and the notion that returning troops deserved easy and free access to the best thought in the civilization they had been fighting for. Recent developments in workplace training, however, reflect more behaviorist notions, wherein the intention is to support specific changes of behavior in employees. Neither of these philosophies is inherently better or worse than another, but they do constitute a major part of the worldview of the educator.

What Perspective Informs Your Teaching?

The second way to examine your underlying assumptions is to start by thinking about the practical details of your teaching. Every educator has a idea about what their teaching should achieve on a concrete level, though we are not always good at explaining what it is. Dan Pratt (1992, 2002) and a number of associates have been working on ways to help educators clarify their position using the Teaching Perspectives Inventory. This online tool requires the educator to answer a number of questions in order to place their practice in terms of these five perspectives:

• *Developmental:* Teaching is seen as being about developing the capacity of the learner to solve more complex problems and deal with more complex ideas. Educators need to start with what the learners already know and work out how to strengthen and deepen it. In learning a musical instrument, for example, learners start with simple exercises and move on to Bach.

• *Apprenticeship:* In this perspective, teaching provides opportunities for learners to learn by doing as much as is possible. Classroom processes try to mimic the demands of the situations in which the learning will be applied. In learning a language, the emphasis would be on participating in conversation rather than learning grammar tables.

• *Transmission:* This perspective focuses on the content and the information, with an emphasis on "getting it across" to the learners. Instructors must be experts in the content, and there is a specific, approved version of the content that must be passed on to learners. In this case, learning a language does involve tables of verbs.

• *Nurturing:* Here the emphasis is on the emotions of the learners and on ensuring that they are comfortable and emotionally committed enough to learn. Learners may be seen as vulnerable, and the role of the instructor is to build the learners' confidence and self-esteem regarding learning. In adult literacy settings, it can be important to ensure that the atmosphere in the classroom is friendly and warm, to counter learners' potential experiences of failure at school.

• *Social reform:* From this perspective, teaching is about supporting changes both within and beyond the classroom or learning setting, and the instructor sets out to facilitate this. In the case of literacy, for example, the emphasis would be on the reasons why some people have valued skills and others do not, rather than the mechanics of using written language.

Pratt and his fellow investigators found that in secondary schooling and college level teaching, the dominant model tends to be transmission. In compiling the results from the one hundred thousand educators who have completed the inventory so far, they discovered that most adult educators have two or three dominant perspectives rather than just one.

The two lists, from Elias and Merriam and from Pratt, have some clear overlaps. One is the social reform perspective and the radical viewpoint, which the writers describe in a very similar way. There are also some very obvious differences. To me, this underlines the point that the values that you attach to education do not necessarily determine your practices. After all, not all humanist educators teach in the same way. This is a useful thing to bear in mind when designing courses— there are many different pragmatic pathways to any given broad and philosophical destination.

Whether you begin at the highest, most philosophical level or investigate your practices more directly through teaching perspectives, I believe you can make several valuable discoveries. The first possibility is looking at your philosophy and your perspective together and seeing how much alignment there is between the two. Most educators will probably find that they pull ideas and values from several different philosophies and perspectives to create their own particular mixture of beliefs and intentions. The interesting question is how consistent these are. If you believe that education is about distributing human knowledge as widely as possible, but you have a nurturing teaching perspective, this will create a certain tension as you try to take care of learners while trying not to "dilute" the content. If you are philosophically humanist but find yourself drawn to a transmission teaching perspective, this will produce other tensions. By starting to understand a little more about the way these levels work together, you can begin to develop an approach to teaching that reflects all you hope to achieve.

The second benefit of looking at your work in these ways is that it can alert you to areas to which you are not paying sufficient attention. For example, if you are a very nurturing teacher, it can be tricky to ensure that you are challenging students sufficiently. If you are very strict about transmission of facts, there may be times when you need to focus on classroom atmosphere and building a welcoming environment. Really, what we need to find is the point of balance between these different perspectives and approaches to our work—one that is both true to who we are and respectful of the learners and the context we work in.

My final point is that thinking through your philosophy and perspective can be a very powerful and effective way to identify the areas you would like to change. If, for example, you would like to be an educator who builds apprenticeship in your classroom, but you find that your dominant perspective is transmission, you can think about what you need to change in order to bring your teaching perspective closer to what you hope for. Which values and intentions do you need to change—and how can you change them?

Philosophies and perspectives hold great potential for providing insights into your educational practices and helping you to plan different ways to do things. Though they can seem abstract, they have powerful concrete consequences for your life and work as an educator. However, you need to take your findings and explore how they can be translated into substantial and sustainable development of your teaching.

WHY IDENTITY MATTERS

In the next chapter I discuss how *learner* identity makes a difference to teaching and learning. One major theme of this book is that your identity as an educator—your life experience, professional background, interests and values—plays a very important role in the way that you approach education. It is important to be clear about who you are and how that makes a difference. In my own case, I am a White heterosexual middle-aged male. People see me in a particular way because of this identity, and there are a number of issues that remain invisible to me because of my identity. I cannot know what it is like to be a woman or a member of a minority in our society. However much I recognize the value of others' experiences in this aspect of life, they are not my experiences. I am strongly aware of the importance of recognizing these gaps and the value of the ways others can address these experiences. If I had to sum up my philosophy of teaching, I would borrow a title from a piece by Michèle Foster (1994): "The Power to Know One Thing Is Never the Power to Know All Things."

I started out working as a community educator in Scotland in the early 1980s. At the time there were deep concerns about unemployment, poverty, poor housing, and drug abuse in what were called "peripheral housing estates." These were enormous swaths of public housing to which people had been moved as the inner-city slums were demolished. There was little money in these communities and typically very few shops or amenities of any kind. My job was to help the people living there to design and build their own recreational resources. The job was challenging, fascinating, and very different from anything I had ever worked at.

Since then I've worked in education for adults in Scotland, Canada, and the United States. I completed a Ph.D. at the University of British Columbia (UBC) that looked at how people set the curriculum in adult learning, and I have followed up with a range of research projects looking mainly at education for adults, though I have made a few dips into schooling from time to time. Recently I've been starting to look at online education because of the recent arrival of Massive Open Online Courses (MOOCs) and the potential for some really interesting opportunities.

Working as a university professor, I still think of myself primarily as an educator of adults. The questions that I face every day are not that different from those I faced in 1983. They revolve around credibility and how to place learners at the center of teaching and learning. I still think a lot about the tendency of educators to impose ideas, or to say what's "right," and how we could handle this better. How can we, in other words, be knowledgeable and have something to offer without drifting into the tendency to act as "experts" and close down the conversation? Teaching still fascinates me because it is so difficult, still, after thirty years.

Values I learned in community education still affect my approach to teaching. These include recognizing that learners have lives outside of the educational process and that things happen that will affect people's engagement with the learning process. I am also concerned with being as equitable as possible. I remain slightly uncomfortable with assigning grades because they often are taken to mean differences in ability rather than in performance. I believe very strongly in diversity as a fundamental characteristic of education, and I remain deeply committed to the idea that education can make things better and bring about the social change we need to address poverty and social injustice.

When I make design decisions in my teaching they are profoundly shaped by my identity and life history, not least by my white privilege. Lund (2010) talks about the benefits that accrue from being a white educator of adults:

> White educators may intellectually acknowledge racism without experiencing or confronting racism. White educators have no responsibility for educating themselves about white privilege and racism. White educators are not required to address racism in the classroom and can still maintain a nonracist image. White educators are not held responsible for learning and understanding about other races and cultures. White educators have the power to distrust and ignore those who bring up racism without recourse. If you are a white educator, your credentials are honored by colleagues and learners. If you are an educator of color, you must prove yourself competent regardless of your credentials. White educators' abilities are respected and anticipated. [pp. 20–21]

The choices made by individual educators, whatever their identity, cannot negate the power of identity in our societies. They can, however, go some way toward changing their manifestation in the specific context in which the educators work. My commitment to social justice leads to an aspiration to find ways to make choices in my teaching that do not perpetuate the dominance of particular groups and ways of thinking, though very often these aspirations are not as well fulfilled as I would like them to be. The most insidious aspect of the privileges I enjoy is the ability to not talk about that privilege, but I believe that those in positions of privilege must not let that possibility stop them from speaking up, however difficult the conversations may be.

When each of us steps into the role of educator, our identity and social position matter a great deal. The same sorts of dimensions I mention in the next chapter when discussing learners apply to educators as well: What is your educational history? What community are you part of, and where is that community situated within your society? How does gender make a difference? What effect does your accent have? The educator can never be a neutral figure.

GOING FURTHER

So far I've laid out some of the factors that potentially make a difference to how educators view their role and put that perspective into practice. In this section I discuss what you can do with this knowledge and how you can use it to improve your teaching by building a map of your abilities and your potential. Earlier in the chapter I introduced the idea that knowing yourself as an educator is comparable to a craftsperson knowing her tools. And just as a woodworker can buy a new chisel, it is possible for educators to expand their tool collection. The more tools are in the bag, the more likely it is that the right implement will be there when you need it. In my view, educators develop by gaining more of these tools and more of the skills needed to make best use of them.

Professional development can be a real challenge for people who teach adults, for a number of reasons. For one thing, adult educators tend to be part-time rather than full-time, and very often they work in sectors that do not require ongoing study for certification. Nurses, for example, have to take a certain amount of training each year to retain their right to practice. If they are asked to become nurse educators in a clinical setting, they still have to keep learning about nursing, but there is no simultaneous expectation that they will study teaching. The same applies to tradespeople, employees of corporations, and even university professors. In most parts of the world, adult educators must voluntarily pursue further training and development. If there were a certification system with expectations for continuing education, it might be easier for educators to ask their employers for time and resources to complete the requirements.

A second and related factor is the pressure of time and work. In England the *Skills for Life* program, designed to enhance basic skills in the population, requires a minimum thirty hours of training every year for educators working within the system. Even for a full-time educator the thirty hours can be hard to spare. In addition, there can often be issues with the range and quality of what is available. Sometimes there may not be thirty hours of high-quality training to sign up for, especially in the third or fourth year of the process.

The National Center for the Study of Adult Literacy and Learning, based at Harvard, conducted a study a few years ago to find out what kind of professional development was most useful to adult educators in terms of bringing about change in practices (Smith, Hofer, Gillespie, Solomon, & Rowe, 2003). Their conclusion, based on an in-depth study of 106 practitioners, was that such changes were very minimal. Seventy-eight percent did report some change, but it wasn't very substantial and was mainly in the way they thought about their everyday class-room practices rather than what they actually did. They found that changes were most likely if teachers were motivated to pursue professional development, had more years of experience, and had a higher level of education. In other words, the more engaged in education the educator was, the more likely he was to change as a result of professional development. Formal professional development is likely to be more useful to those who have education as their main career focus, but most adult educators are not in this situation. So educators need to be careful when selecting professional development, to ensure that it will actually bring about change in practice.

One alternative is for educators to commit to a program of self-development. The danger here is that educators can end up not practicing what they preach, for reasons similar to those just mentioned. Even though adult educators often work hard to support learners to become self-directed, it is not always easy for us to do this for ourselves. People who teach in higher education often have a great many resources available to them, easily and cheaply, but even here there can be a gap between what people would like to do and what they can actually manage. One study (Van Eekelen, Boshuizen, & Vermunt, 2005) found that most instructors learned through interaction rather than self-study. These interactions were equally divided among informal chats with colleagues, discussions with students, and training and planning events. The main point here is that learning, though valuable, was far more often coincidental than part of a master plan.

For people who are interested in changing their practices I offer the following suggestions, based on my own experience and knowledge of the practices of many people working as instructors of adults:

- *Be really clear about what it is you need to learn.* Is it a new technique, an icebreaker, or a different philosophy?

- *It is far easier to start from a concrete problem than from something broader.* So, for example, "How do I help my learners understand the math they need to order the right number of floor tiles?" is a stronger starting point than "How much math should be included in trades programs?"

- *Look for gaps.* If you are aware of the aspects of teaching that worry or challenge you, or leave you wondering how to handle the situation, it is possible to orient your learning toward those parts of your work.

- *Start local*—talk to people around you about what they do to deal with the problems they face. It's quite unlikely that you are the only person to have come across the issue that you are tackling, and even if you do not go along with their solution, it can inform you about what you don't want to do!

- *Consult the library.* There are some excellent books about teaching adults (several are listed in the Further Reading section) that can really be useful here; they are designed to assist with thinking through concrete problems in a really practical way.

- *Look for programs.* Most locations have a wide range of programs in teaching adults available, from single courses to master's and Ph.D. programs. One of the most helpful aspects of these courses can be meeting people in the same situation as yourself.

In the end, it is important that you take responsibility for your own teaching approach and the skills that support it. For most people teaching adults, it is not a full-time job; rather, it is something they do on top of everything else. In this kind of situation, learning comes in small and concrete steps, and your main concern is simply to ensure that those steps are taking you in the direction in which you want to go.

CONCLUSION: PULLING IT TOGETHER

By this point you understand a little about different approaches to teaching adults and why the experience of the educator matters. In concluding this chapter, I suggest some questions that it is useful to be able to answer about yourself as an educator. As mentioned earlier, the answers will not be clear cut and will change with circumstances. So think of this as a process of sketching rather than finishing the masterpiece. It can be useful to know:

- How concerned am I about making sure learners know a certain body of knowledge?
- How important do I believe emotions are in the classroom?
- When and how is it okay to bring social issues into teaching?
- How much of the classroom process should be negotiated with learners?
- How much do I focus on individuals and believe that my role is to help them learn?
- How much do I believe that the classroom is a community that rises or falls together?
- To what extent do I have a body of expert knowledge that needs to be passed on?
- When is it my job to judge how much people have learned?
- How comfortable am I with learners making up their own answers?
- How willing am I to get involved in tensions between students and other classroom relationships?
- To what extent will I be a friend to the students or take on a more traditional professional role?

There are no correct answers to each of these questions. What matters is that you, as the educator, are comfortable and knowledgeable about where you stand on these questions. The more comfortable you are with your own approach, the more effective and responsible your teaching will be and the easier it will be to design the contexts in which you and the learners will thrive. The better you understand what you are trying to do, the more fun you will have doing it.

Engaged and Involved Learners

Learners bring a huge variety of experiences and expectations to learning, influencing both the educational process and the willingness of the learners to get involved in it. No educator can achieve anything without the participation of learners—one of the central skills of education at any level is ensuring that learners are engaged in the process. Sometimes people reply to this claim by pointing out that children do not choose to be in school so they surely cannot be considered willing participants. This is true to some degree, but the mark of a good teacher is to turn *attendance*, which can be required, into *learning*, which cannot. How good teachers do this is one of the great mysteries of education, but we do know quite a lot about the types of factors that make a difference to participation. It's the educator's responsibility to pay attention to these factors and make sure they are addressed. One example that is relevant in many adult education settings is the way that the learners' experience of school affects their comfort and motivation in a classroom, meaning that educators need to think about how the situation can be made more positive for people who do not like education. This is complicated, because many educators enjoyed school (that's why they are educators), whereas adult learners may have had a different experience.

This chapter discusses some of the factors affecting the way learners approach the educational process—factors that necessarily reflect who they are and what kind of experiences they have had in the past. The central design challenge is creating a class process that builds engagement, taking these factors into account. By engagement I mean the involvement and motivation of students with a particular class—so, for example, it can be said that in a mechanics class they are engaged in learning to weld. We will consider the ways educators can help learners direct their energy toward effective learning.

By the end of this chapter you will:

- Be aware of a range of factors that can influence learning and classroom process
- Be prepared to think through how these factors might affect engagement with learning
- Have some ideas about strategies that can help to support engagement

HOW DO PEOPLE LEARN?

One of the first questions that many educators ask when they are learning to teach is how people actually learn and, by extension, how the educator can design situations that help that to happen. There are many theories about this, and having worked with them for some time, I am struck by the fact that these theories seem to fall into several types. Only some of them focus on learning itself. There are some that talk about *why* people learn—although claiming to be about learning, they are really about the reasons that lead people to attend classes. Other theories look at *what* people learn—that is, why certain information and subject areas are attractive at certain times. Both these types of theories are interesting and important, and I discuss them in the next section when I look at learner motivation and engagement.

In the present section I want to look more closely at the question of *how* people learn. It would be really helpful at this point to have some understanding of the process of learning—that is, what structures actually make learning more likely to happen. What, for example, is the process that allows people to go from knowing almost nothing about home decoration to being able to create well-planned living environments for themselves and their friends? How do new employees pick up the explicit and the unspoken knowledge of how to do well in the workplace? When people move to a new country, how does a new language make itself known to them?

There are two very powerful groups of ideas regarding these questions. The first is a cluster of ideas about behaviorism. The central concept they share is that all learning always produces a change in behavior. If you want somebody to ride a bike, the behavioral change that you are looking for is something like "this person can travel safely by bicycle from home to the shops, obeying all traffic laws and operating the machine correctly." Behaviorism is very attractive to many educators, because our actions as educators have demonstrable results and the outcome is absolutely clear. This is different from many other approaches, which to some people can seem very wooly and ill-defined.

Behaviorism was originally developed to provide exactly this precision. Psychology was the same discipline as philosophy until the late nineteenth century, when a group of scientists grew to believe that the use of experimental data might help them to break out of the inward-looking and slightly circular process of philosophizing about the way the mind works. The successes were early and impressive, and by the early twentieth century some ideas had emerged that have since become part of everyday language and thinking. A good example is stimulus-response theory, which suggests that when you provide a stimulus to a person they will react in a certain way (Watson, 1913). By rewarding or punishing these responses, you can train the person to react in a particular way when faced with a set stimulus. The reward or punishment can then be removed in almost every case and the shaped response will continue—in fact, the theory suggests that not rewarding or punishing every response will be more effective, because the person will internalize the process. An example is red traffic lights. Almost all drivers stop at them almost every time, even in the middle of nowhere when there are no police and no visible risks to running them, because we have been trained to respond to the stimulus of the red light by halting, and when we have not stopped, we have usually experienced the disapproval of driving instructors or passengers (or even police officers).

Many educators have understandable concerns about behaviorism. It can appear to reduce humans to machines with no internal life, simply responding to stimuli in the way that has been previously rewarded (Skinner, 1965). Some behaviorist research does seem to suggest this is a fair way to view people, but there is also a range of behaviorist writing that applies the ideas in a humane way and that tackles issues of social justice (for examples, see articles in the journal *Behavior and Social Issues*). Another concern with behaviorism is that learning without an observable outcome simply does not count as learning. This appears to discount learning about the arts in order to develop one's appreciation of aesthetic experience, for example. Although this can be framed as an observable outcome, it's rather clumsy to do so. On balance, these are both reasonable criticisms of behaviorism in its most extreme forms. But the main implications of this approach to learning do not come out of the most radical applications; they are to be found in the central role behaviorist ideas play in typical educational settings.

Behaviorism helps us to understand two aspects of education. The first is that all outcome-based education is based on a behaviorist approach. Just after World War II, Tyler (1949) wrote a very influential book on agricultural education and curriculum development. It was the first popular work to talk about education by objectives, wherein the design of the program flows *backward* from the objectives. Instead of starting the design process with the subject area or the interests of the educator, the idea was to start with what people wanted to be able to do at the end of the course. Tyler wanted learners to be involved in setting the objectives, so his framework was designed not so much to impose a set way of thinking on people as to develop a clear map of the program with them.

The second point is that all assessment is based on behaviorist principles. This seems obvious when we are thinking about learning a concrete skill such as cooking a meal or making a birdhouse. It also applies in more subtle ways, such as the ability to write a three-hour exam on liability law or provide a justified judgment of the quality of a nineteenth-century poem. Unless there is some form of observable activity, there is nothing to assess.

Overall, I think behaviorism provides us with some important and useful tools and does not require human beings to be turned into robots. These tools are not perfect, and they are not useful in every situation. They provide some perspectives that can help with thinking through what we are trying to do as educators and how we will know how we've arrived, but they do not provide much guidance regarding the social aspects of learning. For this, we can turn to another area of theory, called sociocultural learning, which was briefly mentioned in the preface to this book.

Sociocultural learning approaches represent an attempt to understand the ways that people learn from others. This does not have to be direct—there is no need to have somebody literally sitting beside you as you learn. The point is that learning is always social, and it is embedded in our culture and our values. You could argue against this, saying, "I learn best when I'm on my own on a beach, watching the waves and thinking about things." This may be true, but it is really hard for humans to escape the influence of society. Not only are the words we use social constructs, but our entire languages are formed in cooperation with other humans. The way we frame our thoughts is learned, so that even when we watch a natural phenomenon like a wave, the interpretation we give it is based in our shared experience of humanity. This approach to learning underpins my own thinking and, of course, the ideas in this book.

There have been influential developments in this type of approach over the last twenty years or so. The first is the idea of communities of practice. This came out of research in the late 1980s on the way that people learn to perform a variety of tasks such as math (Lave & Wenger, 1991). These studies led to the realization that one really effective way to think about human learning is to use apprenticeship as a model. For any human activity there is a group of people who are really good at it and have been doing it for longer than most people. For example, there is a group of people who are recognized as expert sculptors. They can work in a variety of materials and make a variety of products. If you wanted to commission a costly sculpture for your back garden, these are the people you would go to. They are the sculpture community of practice.

If somebody wants to join a community of practice, she starts off at the edges, trying to gain mastery of some simple abilities (perhaps cutting rocks, in this case). Some people cut rocks on their own, whereas others do it as part of their entry pathway to the community of practice, such as in a class. If it's the latter, which can be generally identified by the intention to join the larger community, it is called "legitimate peripheral participation" (Lave & Wenger, 1991). The person takes part in activities similar to the work of the community of practice but recognized as being at a preparatory level. Over time, the activities get more challenging, and the learner moves toward full membership in the community of practice, making simple structures with easy materials and then moving on to more expressive designs in more challenging media. Another example is student teachers, who start off in field experiences, trying out a few simple things in an established, settled classroom, and over several years moving toward complete responsibility for creating the class.

In this model, learning represents the movement from peripheral participation toward full membership, and it is a dynamic process. As people move further into the community of practice, they become more familiar with the key ways of doing things in that community. However, this should not be seen as simply reproducing the existing sets of practices. It is more about people learning how to use those practices to achieve their own ends. This model of apprenticeship learning is about not only copying established members of the group, but also learning how they do what they do. To continue the sculpture example, the point is not to be able to create the same sculpture as the expert sculptors but to understand what is required for the learner to create her own. For the student teacher, the point is to understand the full range of techniques that can be used with a specific group of students and what the effects are likely to be.

Sociocultural learning supports the use of a problem-based approach to learning (commonly known as problem-based learning, or PBL). This is where the learners are confronted with a challenge that is as authentic as possible and encouraged to work as a group to identify solutions. In the education of doctors it could be a scenario such as "a forty-eight-year old male complaining of toe pain, works as a scaffolder, borrowed work boots from his female colleague." In other contexts there is an endless range of scenarios; for example, in community development in a developing economy the focus could be agricultural or industrial issues. PBL tends to be very popular with learners, in my experience, and it can be a really rich source of learning.

At around the same time that Lave and Wenger were developing their approach, Jack Mezirow (1995) was working on the theory of transformative learning. In this model of adult learning, people possess schema, or ways of looking at the world, that help them make sense of what they see in the world around them. Usually they work quite well, but if things change, the person may face what Mezirow calls a "disorientating dilemma." At this point they not only are open to learning but also *need* to learn so that their world makes sense again. Mezirow argues that the disorienting dilemma is almost always produced and resolved within a specific social context. The examples he gives are deeply concerned with social justice and equity, arising from the differences between the way people think the world should be and the way that they realize it is. So, for example, an individual might believe that an institution is "color-blind" until she sees a person of color being discriminated against; at that point she experiences a dilemma between her belief and her perceptions. The only way to solve such a dilemma, argues Mezirow, is through learning.

To understand how people learn, we can pull these ideas together and produce a highly coherent working model. This does not have the status of a grand theory or explanation, but it may be a helpful way to think about things. Such a model would have these beliefs at its core:

- Learning is a social process conducted, either more or less directly, with other humans.
- People begin to learn by trying peripheral activities, then take on more complex activities as they grow in confidence and see other people perform them.
- Individuals will repeat actions that are associated with a reward, including the approval of peers.
- Even if the aim of the learning is not behavioral, having an associated behavioral outcome can make it easier to communicate and assess.
- People learn most, and most profoundly, when faced with a dilemma or need to understand something relevant to them.

Based on these ideas, it is possible to sketch in a few thoughts about what teachers need to do to support learning. They have to make sure that the point of the learning is clearly communicated to everybody involved and that there is shared understanding of what it means to get there. Educators need to watch for the actions that show that people are starting to move toward the aims of the learning and support those actions. Learners need to have material structured in a continuum from easier ideas and actions toward more challenging ones, so when they have mastered simpler processes they can tackle the more complex ones that build on them (this is referred to as "scaffolding"). The drive in learning is toward understanding and mastery, meaning that educators have to ensure that learners finish the course feeling that they have achieved these two elements.

In the introduction I suggested that responsible teaching recognized the following principles:

- Encourage active learning. People need to learn by *doing* wherever possible, rather than simply hearing or reading about how to do.
- Allow people to have some control over their own learning.

- Build connections between what is being learned and the experiences of learners, moving over time toward more complex ideas.

- Encourage collaboration and conversation between learners.

I hope that the way these principles fit with sociocultural theories of learning makes sense. If you accept the core concepts of the learning theory, these ideas about teaching are the necessary other side of the teaching and learning process.

None of this is particularly complicated or unexpected, and it may well seem obvious to you (especially if you are a parent), but it is sometimes surprisingly difficult to build a course that really reflects these simple ideas. Often we get tangled up with aspects of teaching that aren't necessarily helpful but that take a lot of time, such as conflicts among the learners or unreasonable expectations from employers, and it is easy to feel frustrated and drift away from these ideas toward a model that is more directive and teacher-centered. One of the best possible exercises when that happens is to step back and let a learner lead a segment of the class. Not only will you learn something, but it can also be great reinforcement for the students to see that you trust them to know something about the subject and how to teach it. Supporting learning is not about grabbing onto one theory and hanging on at all costs—it's about pulling together different perspectives to inform the decisions we make with learners. As an educator you will build up your own view of how people learn over time, as you notice things that do and do not work with different groups of people. I am always surprised by the power of learning experiences and the levels of energy people are prepared to put into them. The primary role of educators is to create the relationships and the context that can bring about this type of engagement. In the next section we take a closer look at what engagement means and how it can be fostered.

ENGAGEMENT IN LEARNING

All effective educators hope that learners will get something valuable out of their teaching. For this to happen, learners must be motivated to take an active part in the process rather than sitting back passively and letting the teaching wash over them. This active participation can be summarized in the idea of engagement. Engaged learners listen, talk, respond, reflect, and contribute enormously to the dynamic and the progress of the class. Engagement is not only about the relationship of learners to the subject matter or to the educator; it is also about their relationships with each other. One of the most important concepts in building engagement is that the group of people engaged in learning functions in a holistic way—including the teacher. We really are all in this together.

In this section, I discuss some of the guidelines and ideas that can help to support learner engagement. Educators can help to create the conditions that encourage engagement by learning about—and paying attention to—who the learners are, what they bring to the class, and what they want out of it. While it would be impossible to know exactly what every individual wants, making an effort to understand something about the learners in the class can really help the learning of all involved, including the educator.

As we try to build this understanding, we need to balance generalizations with the characteristics of individual students. Without generalizations educators would be immobilized, as they would have no starting point for designing courses without some sort of broad framework. At the same time, they cannot assume that general approaches will be enough. People are different, however similar their backgrounds and experience might be. Educators who work with adults have been trying for a very long time to understand what adult learners have in common and how they differ from younger learners as well as from each other.

By the 1960s the education of adults was starting to become a profession and academic specialty. Driven by this development, Knowles created the theory of andragogy to provide a framework for teachers of adults. In later years the ideas came to be seen not so much as a theory as a set of assumptions about adults in learning. When first written there were four of these assumptions: (1) people's self-concept changes as they age, from dependence to independence; (2) adults gain a reservoir of experience that can be used in learning; (3) people become ever more ready to learn what they need to know for their social roles; and (4) adults want to learn things that they can apply immediately (Knowles, Holton, & Swanson, 1998). While these are useful ideas, they do strongly reflect the era and the society in which they were written. For example, some feminist writers point out that increasing independence may not be so central to female learners, who may instead seek out and enjoy a richer form of social experience than that offered by a self-determined, highly autonomous approach to life (Tisdell, 1998). Also, Knowles set up the theory of andragogy in direct opposition to the assumptions that drive school teaching. Over the last four decades, education in schools has evolved far beyond what Knowles imagined it to be, and the contrast is not so clear. Nowadays there tends to be more of an acceptance that good teaching is good teaching wherever it is found. So although Knowles's work is still highly respected within education, it is no longer seen as "the answer" to working with adults.

In the 1980s Alan Rogers (1986) provided a list of seven characteristics that he saw as typical of adult learners. Rather than talking about theories of learning or teaching, Rogers presents these as a series of observations based on his own experience, which might look different in different contexts. He says that adult learners:

- *Are adult by definition*, meaning that they choose to be involved in education and they have a greater or lesser sense of self-direction. Educators need to recognize and adapt to this sense of self-direction.

- *Are involved in a continuing process of growth.* There is very little support for the idea that humans stop learning at any point in their lives; adults, just as much as children, are continually faced with new experiences and new perspectives. The teaching provided by educators can be an important aspect of this growth if they are sensitive to the developments people are moving through.

- *Have experience and values.* This is true across the board—whether the teaching concerns a technical skill or interpersonal relationships, adults bring a wide range of history with them. Educators can choose to ignore these factors or even fight them, but they will play out in the learning process. They will affect what is heard by learners, what they feel more or less confident tackling, and whatever less-than-helpful decisions learners make. Learner experience and values can also be an enormously valuable resource, often approached as a set of anecdotes and opportunities for reflection.

- *Usually come to education with set intentions.* This can take the form of either a very precise desire to learn something specific or a vague feeling that the person would like to learn something. Houle (1972) suggests that adult learning can be goal-oriented (interested in learning something specific), learning-oriented (interested in a topic or subject), or activity-oriented (motivated by the process of learning itself). Educators need to understand which of these intentions is at play, because, for example, goal-oriented learners will be very frustrated if they are treated as if they are learning for general interest.

- *Bring expectations about education.* Depending on their experience and previous success in education, these expectations can be extremely positive or more cautious. They may look forward to classes or dread them, be willing to move quickly through material or feel as if they need more support. There is the potential for the educator to lose credibility with the more experienced learners by either taking things too slowly or replicating previous school problems for learners by moving more quickly than expected.

• *Have competing interests.* Most adults involved in learning are not full-time students. They have families, jobs, hobbies, commitments, and worries that are not connected to their learning activities. Although it makes sense to expect a high level of commitment from full-time students who have few other pressing demands in their lives, adult learners are often not in a position to read a great deal outside of class or to attend social activities and workshops. The educator needs to be aware that many adult learners anticipate that a two-hour course will consume exactly two hours per week—expecting too much time and resource commitment from them could lead to stress, conflict, and lower engagement.

• *Have developed set patterns of learning.* Adults continually engage in learning of various types and have developed strategies for doing so. This is influenced in part by their own preferred way of gaining information, which can be reading, listening, working with their hands, discussion, and or any of a number of other methods. In addition, adults may have a preferred pace and sequence of learning (for example, big picture or detail first). One key point to bear in mind is that these will vary across a class. If there are a dozen learners in a class, most likely there will be a dozen different patterns of learning.

A caveat: educators can run into problems by reading lists such as this one and taking them as rules that can be applied to any adult learners, thereby automatically solving challenges of motivation and engagement. These observations will be far more useful if treated as a series of questions concerning learners. So instead of assuming that all adult learners have a strong sense of self-direction, it is important to consider how strong a sense of self-direction each individual learner has and how the educator can respond to it. In addition, it is important to consider the extent to which adults can autonomously choose not to exercise their self-direction. Sometimes adult learners want lots of support in their learning, creating a bit of a dilemma for an educator who wants to support self-determination. The key point is for the educator to think through these factors and to be aware that they matter a great deal.

Haggis (2002) conducted research with a group of adults who were returning to graduate school study. She wanted to find out how the assumptions of adult learning approaches such as andragogy actually fit the learners, as she was struck by the extent to which they were promoted as universal and accurate in different contexts. Haggis found that the one characteristic adult learners shared was enormous diversity in terms of their attitudes and approaches to learning. Some were highly self-directed, others far less so. Some people wanted to learn things they could apply immediately; others were much more interested in learning for its own sake. Based on this research, she argued that the most important thing to take into account when working with adults was not so much any particular factor or approach to learning, but the diversity of approaches they bring.

One way to think about engagement is an approach called "learning careers" (Crossan, Field, Gallacher, & Merrill, 2003). This perspective emphasizes the continuity of learning activity across a person's life rather than dividing it into initial education, work-based training, and individual study, for example. It accepts that people's learning experiences (including periods when they are not involved in formal learning) accumulate to create a lifelong picture of learning, just as the various types of work that people are involved in accumulate to create a work career. And just like work careers, learning careers will be different for everyone.

Careers in this sense will not be linear and "upward," as we might traditionally expect with employment. Rather, they are complex stories of getting more or less engaged in learning over time, influenced by friends, family, opportunities, and barriers. Making sense of them means accepting that some decisions can be made by individuals, but others are beyond their control. In addition, they imply that people have a range of goals and pathways through work, life, and learning that evolve as they become older. "Learning careers" is a shorthand way to summarize all the diverse trajectories, loops, and curves that bring people to work with you in the classroom.

This framework provides a way to remind ourselves that the learners in the class have been brought there by a range of different learning experiences, and that the work of the educator will have different meaning for different people because of these diverse careers. There is some evidence that learning careers are a good concept for capturing many of the factors that affect engagement (Field, 2009). The idea of learning careers makes sense to many learners, and it can often be openly discussed within the group or individually. It is a nonthreatening and intuitive way to explore people's history and circumstances and the way these have influenced their learning. Acknowledging the importance of learners' backgrounds in this way may be a very effective start to building engagement.

One simple and often very effective way to start the conversation is to ask people to draw a line on a large sheet of paper to represent their learning career. This can have dates across the top and the bottom to help organize the diagrams, but this is optional. In either case, you will be surprised by the results of this exercise. There will be loops and dotted lines and gaps and places where the line is made heavier to show a period of intense learning. If you set it up as all learning, not just formal learning, you will perhaps be struck by how much learning can be associated with difficult life events such as the end of relationships or illness (rather like the transformative learning ideas mentioned in the previous section). It is important that the educator completes this exercise as well and is comfortable taking part in the conversations that come out of the diagrams.

After doing this with several classes (and obviously there are occasions where it is not possible or appropriate), it becomes second nature to view learners as people with complex histories and great levels of experience and knowledge. It also helps to dispel the subconscious assumption that people learn in linear ways, moving through school systems in an orderly fashion. So many of the conversations about education focus on the formal schools and issues such as "drop-outs" that are actually about people stepping outside that formal system and not about rejecting learning. When working with adults, it is clear that people take very different routes to their goals, and that people often do find a way to participate in the educational experiences they need, even if not in conventional ways.

The learning careers approach can also help to build relationships between students, by providing a mechanism to share life histories and to ask each other questions about them. Common experiences will be discovered, and there are often comments such as "I wish I'd done that. I want to hear all about it!" It can make it easier for learners to discuss the ideas and challenges of the class, as they have some understanding that they have all followed winding paths to end up working together. Quite often it can also help to underline the point that an individual's history may not be a barrier to learning. There can be a sense that if the learners with the most complex histories can be here after all the challenges of their life and be successful, then other folks can be too. Confidence rises, and with it comes participation and that elusive energy that makes courses work.

In conclusion, engagement is a critical concern for educators. If people are not interested and motivated, there is very little the teacher can do. Many of the skills of working with adults entail supporting and maintaining a high level of engagement. Teachers working with adults do start with one great advantage: in most cases adults choose to attend courses, unlike school children. This means that they usually walk in the door highly receptive to what class has to offer, and the challenge for the educator of adults is to maintain that receptiveness. The flip side of adults' ability to choose to be there, of course, is that usually they can also choose not to be there, which is a huge challenge for longer courses involving intense study, such as adult literacy. Making sure that the learners have had an opportunity to engage with you as instructor, with the topic, and with their colleagues can make it that much easier for them to persevere.

LEARNER DIVERSITY

Individual learning careers bring individuals to the course, but who people are and what they have done both make a significant difference in the learning process. Some of the factors affecting this are unique to the individual, but a range of the most influential factors is rooted in social experience. Not all educators or learners will be comfortable acknowledging all of the factors that matter, which include ethnicity, gender, and sexuality, as well as social class (Merriam & Caffarella, 1999). Yet these aspects of individuals' identity will profoundly affect their expectations of the class, of you as an educator, of the other learners, and of the process. As discussed in the previous chapter, the identity of the educator also matters here, and not in a simple way. Sometimes, for example, a male educator will have an advantage in working with male students, but this is not always true. These dynamics are often very hard to discern and predict, particularly if they concern issues of power and resistance. An individual's learning career may have persuaded him that male educators should not always be trusted, for example, and this will not always be obvious to the teacher who is newly working with this person.

In the previous chapter I touched on the question of the privilege that the educator may enjoy. It is often very important to take this into account. As Rocco and West (1998) argue, "if we do not reflect upon the assumptions that create privilege, the current power structures will be reproduced, but with different targets as demographics change" (p. 172). This does not mean that educators have to explicitly engage in discussing the issues with learners, which could be uncomfortable for all involved. What it does mean, in my view, is that the presence of privilege should be acknowledged when making decisions about design. Diversity is always present, and it always matters, and the role of the educator is to work out the best way to acknowledge and respond to it. The most unacceptable option is to pretend that it doesn't play a part in your teaching. At the very least, responsible educators should be working to create opportunities for different forms of engagement and diverse types of learning that may not always fit their expectations but that represent highly authentic learning.

It would be unfair to expect educators to be able to deal with every possible variation of learning career and to resolve issues that may well go back to individuals' earliest experiences with education. However, it is reasonable to expect that they will be conscious of these issues and sensitive to the wide range of effects they may have in the teaching and learning process. For example, the understanding of education brought by learners who belong to an ethnic minority depends on the history of their community, their own learning careers, and the place of their community in the broader society. All learners come both as individuals and as representatives of a particular history, and it is important for educators to recognize the existence of these nuances, although they cannot be experts in every possible type of diversity.

There is a lot of research on the ways that different types of diversity matter in education. Some of the earliest work looked at gender and ethnicity; examination of the meaning of sexuality in the class has taken a little longer to develop. These wide-ranging and informative analyses constitute some of the most insightful and interesting research on teaching and learning. Given the space limitations of this section, I strongly recommend that educators follow up and do some reading on these topics. As humans, we have a tendency to generalize from our own experience, and it can be informative and refreshing—and often necessary—to step beyond our own perspective.

Although finding information about how diversity may affect education is fairly straightforward, it is far harder to find recommendations for what to do about it. As in our earlier discussion of generalizations, the difficulty is that broad statements may be helpful but just as often may not be. They may simply reinforce stereotypes. It may be that a working-class learner has had a rocky educational history because of differences between their values and those of the institutions they have attended, but it's equally possible that this has not been their experience. Working with diversity is one of those areas that most profoundly challenges the sensitivity of educators and their ability to work in a responsive way with learners. In this section I set out some of the main ideas related to age, gender, ethnicity and culture, class, sexuality, and learning diversity. Then I identify common elements that are important to think about in our teaching and point to some ways of approaching these issues that I hope will be helpful.

Any discussion of diversity has to begin by acknowledging that for a very long time the diversity found among learners was not taken into account in education. There seems to have been a long tradition of assuming that learners were identical, or at least very similar. There was no explicit assumption that all students would be pre-middle-aged Anglo-Saxon males with a good command of English, but this was so only because it seems to have rarely occurred to anybody designing education that the identity and background of learners might matter. Behind the scenes there was an assumption that the knowledge, experiences, and values of the European man was the common ground on which learning could be built. The explosion of interest in other ways of approaching the world and understanding learning in the last fifty years represents a profound shift in views of education.

It is perhaps unsurprising that age is one major form of diversity acknowledged in adult education. When an educator is working in a school, age is generally not an issue. The children's ages may vary by a year or two but they generally are very similar in their outlook and experience. When educators are working with a wide range of ages—from people beyond retirement age to individuals who have just left school—the differences are often substantial. A lot of the early thinking about working with older learners was that (1) they were likely to be less interested in work-related learning because they were advanced in their careers, and (2) it would be more difficult for them to learn. The first of these assumptions seems to contain some truth, though the data available is not always as reliable as it could be (Sargant & Aldridge, 2002). The second, however, can be confidently dismissed. There is some evidence that the way people learn things changes to some degree as they age, but there is no reason to assume that any individuals at any age cannot learn anything they want to learn.

The view that the older years of human life have to be viewed as a time of decline (with different rates of descent for different people) is such an ingrained perspective that it can be hard to move beyond it. There is no doubt that older people may be more likely to be facing physical challenges to learning, such as less acute hearing, but this is a specific organic issue and not a global barrier to learning. There are strong arguments for resisting the way that older adults are approached in Western society and moving toward a social justice orientation in their education (Findsen & Formosa, 2011). In this way, we can regard older adults as having much in common with any other group that has been oppressed by conventional educational thinking.

It seems to me that it is important for educators working with adults to develop some expertise concerning age-related factors, as these are so much a hallmark of our work. One example of a concrete effect is called "cohort consciousness." If you are working in a trades education program—say, in masonry—there could be a wide range of ages of learner in the class. The span could easily be from twenty to fifty years of age. Knowing that everybody in the room has to be a high school graduate, it might be tempting to assume that everybody will start learning from the same point. But the fifty-year-old will potentially have graduated from high school long before the twenty-year-old. This has two implications: first, the curriculum leading to high school graduation will have changed over that span of thirty years; second, high school math could well be thirty years more distant for the fifty-year-old than it is for the twenty-year-old. Not only will the content be different, but they will also have a different relationship to it.

The other side of the argument is that the fifty-year-old will have a great deal more experience and will have learned a range of pragmatic ways of doing things, whereas the twenty-year-old may believe, based on school experience, that there is one way to get the right answer. When learners are seen in this way, in terms of the learning career appropriate to their cohort experience, the educator can begin to recognize that there are ranges of complementary experience and knowledge within the group of learners.

Diverse cohorts may well have different relationships with computers. Stereotypically, younger learners are often thought of as much more ready to use the Internet and computers to support their learning in other ways. This is probably not as accurate a generalization as it once was, but it is generally helpful to be aware that different ages of learners may use computers in different ways. Twenty-year-olds are more likely to know about social media and to have used it in their lives, for example. The focus of computer use in classrooms is shifting from different levels of technology use to different uses among groups.

Another critical dimension of difference in adult learning contexts is gender. This is a more profound issue than many people realize, as there is good evidence that men and women tend to have substantially different approaches to learning. This is not necessarily a "natural" difference, but it does show up in many societies. A great deal of work on human development in the middle of the twentieth century was based on the premise that people become more autonomous and self-determined as they go through their lives (Perry, 1970), as can also be seen in Knowles' theory. It follows that a lot of research into adult learning has started with the same sort of assumptions, using them to shape program design and intended outcomes. However, work by feminist scholars around thirty years ago challenged these assumptions by demonstrating that many women view the world in a different way than men do. Instead of aiming for an ideal form of independence, the women studied tended to value interconnectedness and mutual reliance and were able to describe a different way of knowing about the world (Belenky, Clinchy, Goldberger, & Tarule, 1997; Gilligan, 1982).

These two pieces of research, which were sophisticated and convincing, generated many follow-up studies. In this body of work, the life experiences of women have been explored in detail, and the way these experiences affect their learning have been described. The evidence builds up to a strong argument that the challenges faced by women in adult learning often differ from those faced by men. On the broadest level, women still perform the majority of domestic and caring labor and are paid less than men for the same work. For example, the vast majority of single parents are female. Yet women are at least as likely as men to be involved in education (McGivney, 1999), suggesting that women find learning valuable despite the difficulties they face. One possibility is that women have fewer chances to study in early adulthood and are more likely to return to education later in life. However, the type of learning that women engage in is typically different from men's choices. A good example is adult literacy, where commonly the majority of learners are female even though the tested skill levels of women and men are very close.

One recent report looking at UNESCO global adult education initiatives makes it clear that although the policy supports addressing women's learning as a political priority, the situation on the ground is very different (Stromquist, 2013).

The writer argues that education for women is still largely invisible around the world, even more so because it often takes place in informal rather than formal settings. The current political trends push toward recognition of formal education for productivity rather than any broader concept of what education could be, reinforcing the lack of status and visibility experienced in less formal settings, such as education for women.

Although it is not helpful to generalize and say that all women see things in one way and all men see them another, we can say with some confidence that women and men often have different perceptions of what is happening in a classroom or other learning situation and how they are relating to those processes (Beer & Darkenwald, 1989). Whether the educator is male or female, there is a good possibility that the educator may not be picking up on these nuances. Hayes (1989) says that traditional educational models have not really met the educational needs of women, and that models of learning and teaching that address both individual development and social change may work better. It's not realistic to expect that all education delivered to adults can include these elements, but it is a useful reminder of the extent to which traditional education has not recognized the ways in which women's learning careers are different from men's. Sensitivity to the issues of gender as they are experienced by different learners is a key asset for educators.

The educational implications of cultural and ethnic background are equally complex to think through. Discussion of ethnicity in adult education often focuses on people who are not White, making people of Northern European descent the norm against whom all others are considered. The majority of the research addresses African-American experiences in the United States. It is important to bear in mind that African-Americans have experienced a remarkably high level of overt oppression for several centuries within a certain social context. Although ethnicity always matters, it is likely to have varying significance depending on the specific context.

I do want to be clear that ethnicity is *not* directly related to learning ability. There is no credible evidence that two children growing up in the same environment would differ in any significant way just because one had Indigenous North American heritage and the other had African-American heritage. No one area of the world produces people that are *inherently* better or worse at learning anything than any other area. The differences in learning career that people experience comes from social—and not physical—causes.

The theories concerning ethnicity in education have evolved a great deal over the last ten years. In the early 2000s there was considerable interest in Afrocentrism and its implications for African-American learners and instructors (Hunn, 2004). Current analyses have expanded on this earlier work and are now examining differences and commonalities between the experiences of different marginalized communities (Hughes & Berry, 2012). Although oppression of certain people on the grounds of their identity remains at the center of the conversation, there is growing recognition that the situation cannot be reduced to one dimension. Instead, there is acknowledgment that the experiences of groups and individuals vary a great deal. There is some excellent scholarship on the way that critical race theory, a relatively new body of work on these issues, can help to inform how we work with diverse adult learners (Closson, 2010).

In terms of pragmatic program design, it seems to me that two aspects of cultural difference are worth considering. First, different cultures have different orientations to learning, including how learning can happen and what it means. There are many aspects of difference in the way cultures, from the national level all the way to the most local, view the logistics and process of learning. Some cultures value talking as an equal with instructors, whereas others prefer the instructor to retain some distance from the learners and act as an expert. In some cases, men and women are expected to be taught in different locations. People who answer the teacher's questions can be seen as showing off in some settings, whereas in others it is a mark of respect. Book learning can be seen as vital and valuable in certain contexts and less important than practical experience in others.

The second aspect is the way that learners from different backgrounds are treated by educational institutions. As one writer on home-school relationships in the United States (Auerbach, 2007) puts it:

> The unequal distribution of economic, human, cultural, and social capital. . . constrain parents' involvement options, inclinations, and relations with schools . . . African American and Latino parents are more likely than those of the dominant culture to have a skeptical, ambivalent, and potentially adversarial stance toward school programs that have historically failed their communities. [p. 252]

In other words, at the level of schooling, minority families have not been served well, and this has created a caution about schooling that will continue well beyond the age of leaving school. Somebody who has been treated in a stereotyped way at school, whether negatively or positively ("you must be good at x because you are a y"), will not always find it easy to enter a classroom as an adult. In my experience (as a White man working mainly in Western nations), some learners appreciate having this acknowledged, but others do not. Again, as with gender, it is important to avoid "essentializing" learners by assuming that they will feel a specific way about some aspect of learning because of who they are. These assumptions can be seen as "microaggressions" by learners, perpetuating the biased views of participants that lead to justified disengagement (Solorzano, Ceja, & Yosso, 2000).

Despite the complex relationship between minority groups and formal education systems in various parts of the world, many of these groups value learning very highly. Surveys conducted in the UK (Tuckett & Aldridge, 2008; Jones, 2010) show that people from visible minority backgrounds participate more in adult learning than those from majority backgrounds and are more likely to be studying toward a qualification rather than for leisure reasons. This suggests that studying later in life to reach a specific goal is relatively common in minority communities and that educators have a responsibility to ensure that the setting is welcoming and comfortable for all learners, whatever their careers up to that point.

Before leaving gender and ethnicity, I would like to bring in some concrete ways in which work with historically marginalized learner groups may differ from traditional education. Leicester (2001) identified seven characteristics that have emerged mainly from feminist scholarship and that she believes are important to consider when working with many different groups of learners:

- Learning is personal.
- The teaching and learning process must recognize emotional intelligence and intuitive understanding.
- Wholeness, balance, and integration are important themes.
- There should be an emphasis on networks and communication.
- Values are important.
- The bicultural advantage that learners have gained through familiarity with both the mainstream culture and their own is important.
- Many groups possess enormously rich survival skills that can be a key resource for learning.

By bringing characteristics such as these into course design, we can begin the process of opening up learning to the diverse experiences of learners.

As with ethnic and cultural identity, the social class of learners affects their learning career in different ways in different contexts. There is a striking difference in the amount of attention paid to this issue in different places. In European studies of adults learning, the social class of adults in terms of their occupational status is almost always considered; in North American studies it rarely is (Nesbit, 2006). This is an important omission, since socioeconomic status (SES) makes a very significant difference to learning.

There are two effects of socioeconomic status that may be most relevant to education for adults. The first begins in early learning. There is a great deal of evidence that children from lower SES groups do not do so well in the first years of schooling. One report states that at the age of seven, children from lower SES groups are outperformed by over 30 percent by children from upper SES groups (Sabates, Feinstein, & Skaliotis, 2007). These early differences can affect an individual's entire learning career, especially in school systems that divide children into different tracks at an early age. Second, SES profoundly affects the likelihood of people being involved in learning as adults, with one report stating that 17 percent of adults in the upper two SES bands have not studied again since leaving school, compared to 58 percent of adults in the lowest two bands (Sargant & Aldridge, 2002). This is strong evidence both for the importance of SES to learning and for the value of considering learning careers over time.

It is challenging and important to offer educational opportunities to learners from lower SES backgrounds, and the history of adult learning is marked with a strong interest in issues of class. Some of the earliest adult education organizations around the world were set up to ensure that working people had access to the same knowledge as the more privileged. When I started working in Scotland in the early 1980s, social class and associated issues such as poverty were seen as the primary focus for education among adults, in the hope that awareness of significant social divisions would lead people to come up with solutions. Currently such issues are less prominent in the intentions of adult learning organizations, but they still matter, and often in a concrete way. As Nesbit (2006) argues, most studies of class in adult learning focus on the ways that working class adults exclude themselves from education, leaving untold the stories of people from lower SES groups who do engage in learning. There is evidence that there is a distinctive working-class learning style that is collective, mutual, and solidaristic, using the rich cultural background that these groups can bring to learning. In other words, having a working class background may lead to ways of learning that are effective but that may not fit too well with formal systems.

Another point to bear in mind when working with people whose learning career reflects a lower SES background is that their experiences may affect their confidence (Joseph Rowntree Foundation, 2007). People who do not have a middle-class background often expect that their culture and experiences will be viewed as unimportant by an educator, and it can be an important role for teachers of adults to help these learners to "unlearn" this expectation. One key component of this is being as clear as possible about expectations. I was the first person in my family to move beyond secondary education, and I still remember how confusing educational culture was to me, whether in formal or informal settings. A simple explanation of what was going to happen, how, and when, would have gone a long way.

One significant form of diversity that educators will encounter is sexuality. There has been emerging interest in this aspect of identity in education generally, and within education for adults this has led to research using Queer Theory to understand learners' experiences. The first point to note is that sexuality can be profoundly diverse, including straight, lesbian, gay, transgendered, bisexual, intersexual, and two-spirited identities (Grace & Wells, 2007). Unlike other forms of diversity, sexuality is not necessarily visible or audible, but it can be a powerful force in the classroom. Educators can react subtly to their perception of learners' sexuality in ways that represent microaggressions. For example, do educators omit materials that show people of all sexualities in a positive light? Do they include materials that show them in a negative light? Sexuality is one of the areas where people often feel comfortable making jokes about others; is the instructor either doing this or allowing it to happen in the class? One of the key points here is the importance of not assuming that all learners or instructors are heterosexual (Gunn, 2010), or that everybody has a partner of the opposite gender. There is a growing body of evidence that the learning careers of sexual minorities will have been affected by their identity, and once more the responsibility of the educator is finding ways to use these experiences as resources for learning.

Finally, I would like to comment briefly on learning ability and disability. In the education of adults there is a tendency to be wary of the idea of learning disabilities and to accept that people have all sorts of effective approaches to learning. This philosophy fits very well with the idea of universal design, which sets out to create environments and process that are as accessible as possible to everybody (Burgstahler, 2012). The aim of universal design is to remove the barriers to participation, requiring educators to ensure that every challenge facing participants stems from the learning that is being asked of them and not from the environment. A straightforward example concerns people with limited visual acuity. If they sit at the back of the room, it may be hard for them to read words on a screen. It is not complicated to either invite them to sit closer to the front or to provide everybody with a paper or electronic version of materials in advance of the presentation. As with many of the issues facing educators, the challenge is not so much finding solutions as it is striving to be more conscious of the potential problems.

As well as finding different things easier or more difficult to learn, people also have preferences for the way they like to receive new information. Some people like pictures, others texts, and still others prefer discussing ideas. This is the basis for the idea of learning styles. I believe it is necessary to be cautious about these ideas because they can put learners into boxes. People may prefer information in different forms at different times on different topics. They may soak up visual data on math and find it really hard to learn carpentry from pictures. Overall, I believe strongly that the best response for the educator is to provide information and arrange the class process to include as many variations as possible. This allows people to respond in different ways to the ideas brought forward and to find a variety of pathways to engage with them. The educator's skill lies in taking something people are not aware of and making it clear to the widest possible range of people.

In this section I have tried to provide a few preliminary insights into the sorts of dynamics that educators of adults may come across. Of course, these different aspects may come together and cut across each other in complicated ways. It is perfectly possible to have an economically privileged person from a visible minority group sitting next to a working class person from the majority group. These different factors play out not in simple or easily controlled ways but in complicated configurations. I have not really discussed the social significance of these different factors, which can make a huge difference in learning. But it seems to me that a single educator cannot tackle all of the discrimination and oppression that have previously affected the learning careers of the learners. What the educator can do is work to ensure that these experiences are not continued. In the next section I discuss one approach to achieving this.

RESPONDING TO DIVERSITY

Effective adult educators tend to take the diversity of learners seriously and acknowledge that they are different from each other as well as from the educator. Whether in terms of addressing the different ways people like to learn, the culture of the learners, their class background, their gender, or a range of other aspects, the educator has a responsibility to respond to the varying learning careers of the people they work with. Ignoring the differences and treating everybody the same can seem like a good option, suggesting a democratic equality and lack of prejudice against, or in favor of, any group. The problem with this approach is that people do not enter the classroom on an equal footing, so treating them equally within it (even if that were really possible) simply continues the existing advantages and disadvantages. If two people are equally good runners and one is given a ten-second head start, that one will always win, regardless of whatever pains are taken to make sure that they run at the same speed once they are both moving. The same thing applies in learning, with one important difference: we would like people to reach the finishing tape at about the same time after having covered the same ground.

One of the most powerful actions an educator can perform in this situation is to take on the role of learner. Although the teacher may be the expert on the subject area covered in the class, the learners are the experts on the learning careers that have brought them there. One possible response to diversity is to be genuinely open to learning about the various aspects brought to the specific setting by all the people there. This means that some time must be spent in framing the learning process together with the learners. As suggested in the discussion of engagement, it can be really helpful to have a set of questions to explore together with learners to reach some form of mutual understanding of the purpose and process of the class.

The educator is challenged to be aware of the way social and identity factors play out in learning without becoming fixated on them or assuming that they explain everything. We should not assume, for example, that all White learners have had an easy or privileged pathway through education. Although one factor may have tended to make things easier for them in some contexts, there is a range of other factors about which the educator knows little. So how do educators manage a discussion so that they can learn about learners and the learners can get a know a little about each other and the instructor? It can be very effective to focus a session on people's views of learning. Instead of looking at individuals' entire learning careers and their identity and then trying to deduce what kind of educational approach would work for them, be pragmatic: talk about what sort of expectations people have and how they can be fulfilled. Consider asking people to comment on:

- A time when they learned something in a really satisfying way
- How much time they can devote to work outside the class (if necessary)
- What sort of balance between group work, lecturing, and workshops sounds right
- What they expect to leave the program being able to do
- What sort of ground rules for behavior and discussion are important

Over time, educators will build up their own range of important questions to ask in their own classes to provide the insights they need. New educators may be concerned that asking these questions will make them appear unsure of what they are doing, but I believe very strongly that working with learners to identify the processes that are most effective and most respectful of learners' preferences is a hallmark of capable educators who take their role seriously. It allows for recognition of individuals' cumulative learning careers on a very practical level without asking learners to expose themselves and talk about their experiences in detail.

A very similar approach has been gaining ground in schools, where there is also a need to take into account the diverse backgrounds of learners. Two streams of thought are coming together: (1) "culturally responsive teaching," which sets out to respond directly to cultural and linguistic diversity among students; and (2) "differentiated instruction," which sets out to respond to learners of different abilities (Santamaria, 2009). Even though these ideas came about for different reasons that are important to differentiate (learners working in a second language are not in the same position as learners who are struggling in their first), their approaches to learner diversity are highly compatible. For the purposes of this discussion, I'm going to consider these ideas together and call the approach "responsive teaching."

One aspect of responsive teaching is providing the same content at different levels of complexity. When you are teaching history, for example, one group of learners may be working on the narrative of a specific event while others are analyzing the event in terms of its relationship to others and the larger ideas behind both. One group will be learning about the sequence of events of the 1770s and 1780s while the other is uncovering the intellectual environment that made these two decades the most revolutionary period in modern history. Because group interaction and getting students of diverse backgrounds working together are also important principles, ultimately all the learners will end up covering the same concepts in the same depth. Assessment will be varied across students, with the key requirement that learners demonstrate that they are being active and responsible in dealing with the subject matter (Tomlinson, 1999). Project-based work and peer mentoring could be useful ways to incorporate this idea, including learner-led presentations of work in forms that they select to allow for different ways of showing their engagement. One learner might choose a formal presentation, another a short video, a third the development of an online resource.

There is also an important social element to this work. Many forms of diversity are not inherent in learners but have been built up from social experiences over the years, and educators need to consider how much they want to tackle some of these issues in the classroom. This will vary by context and topic to some degree, but there are still important choices regarding how openly issues need to be brought up. I believe that many educators understand that education should be an opportunity for people to develop their critical skills, including the ability to assess evidence and make up their own mind about things. The tricky bit is knowing how to do this without imposing the educator's views on the learners. For example, in my own teaching I try to get people to consider and potentially challenge commonsense notions of gender roles, but taking this step effectively means making it clear where I stand (after all, if I were comfortable with traditional gender roles, why would I even bring it up?). Being open about convictions without being judgmental can be difficult, but it is often useful to provide students with materials that allow them to at least explore different views on key ideas in a nonthreatening way. So, for instance, a literacy class could look at 1950s advertising as a safer way to explore the representation of women (see Figure 2.1).

Figure 2.1
A Particularly Dated 1950s Advertisement for Dacron
(© Dacron Leggs)

The diversity of experiences learners bring can be used as resources for learning. For example, an opportunity to discuss people's neighborhoods and the way the residents interact can be an important reinforcement of social science concepts. In teaching a subject like mechanics, for example, many learners will have experience with trying various tasks on their own vehicles and can tell stories of successful—and not so successful—attempts. In adult literacy classes, learners often know how to recognize different words in various languages, making it possible to create a shared multilingual vocabulary. Rather than focusing on what learners cannot do, this can be a really powerful way to emphasize the competencies they already possess and can share with their peers and the instructor.

When the educator is creating groups of learners to work together in this kind of framework, the groups do not have to consist of people who are all the same. It can be very effective to assemble different types of learners with a variety of learning careers into a group to work on a project. Their range of ways of learning ideas and expressing them adds richness to the process for all involved and can often lead to results that pleasantly surprise the instructor.

Recognizing the many forms of invisible and visible diversity when working with adult learners can sound like a lot of work, especially in a situation where specific objectives have to be reached. There are two things to bear in mind here. First, the principle of responsive teaching is concerned with all learners making progress toward similar goals but allowing the development of various pathways to get there (McTighe & Brown, 2005). The educator does not have to personally develop each of these pathways but can instead create opportunities for them to develop and can support them when they do. Second, learning to be an educator is a long developmental process involving the accumulation of a toolbox of strategies. If we take responsive teaching seriously, we create that toolbox with diversity in mind rather than a "one size fits all" approach. This does not necessarily require more skills; it simply requires different skills. Instead of having a range of ways to support learners to do well on a test, for example, the responsive educator has a range of different ways to demonstrate learning. In the case of literacy, for example, this could mean recognizing a learner's expertise in community language literacy rather than school-based forms of reading and writing.

The recognition of learners as full and informed participants in the learning process has been one of the remarkable aspects of the education of adults since its inception. There has long been a philosophical commitment to ensuring that learners are not treated as empty vessels waiting to be filled with knowledge, but instead are approached as people with their own knowledge, experiences, and history. The most widely cited educational writer in the world, Paulo Freire, was deeply concerned with this issue. Coming from a radical social change viewpoint, he worked through what this would mean for the teaching and learning process. His most influential work, *Pedagogy of the Oppressed* (1971), lays out a practical method for recognizing and validating the knowledge of learners. The design challenge that continues to face every educator of adults is knowing how to do this is a profound and effective way, moving beyond simple acknowledgment of diversity toward the type of recognition that builds and maintains engagement in learning.

CONCLUSION: MAKING DIFFERENCE MATTER

In this chapter I have covered a lot of ground regarding the way the learner experience can vary and how it can affect the process of learning. I hope the message coming through is that although it is important for educators to recognize these differences, you do not need to know everything (if such a thing were even possible). I believe the role of the educator is to actively and deliberately create the space to allow diversity to emerge. The practical steps needed to accomplish this are not necessarily complicated. They entail listening to learners and offering options in response to the insights they share. This approach does not minimize difference or deny its importance; rather, it offers a principle for developing and organizing pragmatic strategies to ensure that diversity is present in the learning process.

In the later chapters of this book I will look in more detail at the ways learner identity and diversity play out in various aspects of the educator's work, with a continued focus on pragmatic responses. I hope that this chapter has been helpful in emphasizing the importance that these factors have in our work with adults. These are not easy things to think about, but as educators we have a responsibility to step beyond that discomfort in order to support effective learning that engages students. Recognition of learning careers and the diversity that feeds into them is very strongly motivating for learners, making them feel that they belong and that they have something to offer as well as something to take away. This can go a long way to creating the group dynamic of engagement and commitment that under-pins both enjoyment and effectiveness in adult learning.

chapter THREE

Context Drives Design

I n the last two chapters we looked at the way your identity and history as an educator and the learning careers of participants affect the learning process. In this chapter I turn to the context in which learning and teaching occur. Context is not just a container for the education process—it is a powerful influence on the design of education. As Cervero and Wilson (1994) put it, "because education is a practical art, program planners are judged by how well they deal with concrete planning situations in which they have a specific group of learners (not the generic adult learner), a specific organizational context, and limited resources of money and time" (p. 19).

The first section of this chapter looks at the research on the influence of context, which fits very well with the sociocultural theory we are using to frame learning. In the rest of the chapter I will discuss different aspects of context, starting with questions around the formality of the context and the use of technology. Other aspects of the context are the organization you are working for, the type of course it is, the time that is available, and, finally, the physical setting. This last section touches on the resources for teaching that are available in the specific context, which I will return to in more detail in Chapter Five. This is a wide range of topics, but they are tied together by the need for educators to understand the environment in which they are working.

By the end of this chapter you will:

- Be aware of the deeply contextual nature of education and learning
- Know how context can make a difference to your work
- Be able to see how your work fits in its context

WHY CONTEXT MATTERS

Context matters a great deal in the education of adults. Over the last twenty years or so there has been increasing interest in adult learning and the effects of context—in other words, how knowledge is built by people in particular places at particular times in conjunction with other people. The context is not "around" the learning, it is at the heart of it. The great breakthrough of the last two decades has been the realization that pretty much all human learning works in that way. The recognition of context as a fundamental attribute of knowledge has been one of the most important evolutions in learning in recent times. As Hansman (2001) puts it, "learning in context is paying attention to the interaction and intersection among people, tools, and context within a learning situation" (p. 44).

Interest in the role of context can be traced back to the Soviet psychologist Vygotsky (1978). Among the many insights he brought to education was the interesting observation that people can do more in a group than they can alone. He called this difference the Zone of Proximal Development, meaning it was the area in which the person was most deeply engaged in the process of learning. For example, if you are learning to ski, there will be some steep slopes that you really do not want to tackle alone but that you will follow a friend down. Eventually you will master the slope and do it alone. Vygotsky's notion that humans construct knowledge and ability through working with others is a crucial challenge to the idea that learning is something that individuals do alone and in their heads. It pushes us to think about the ways in which we work as groups and communities to achieve our aims, and the importance of the human context as we do so.

One sociocultural perspective, called social learning theory, has produced some important insights into supporting people to learn in contexts such as health education (Evans, 1989). This theory suggests that learning, in the sense of adopting new behaviors, comes about through modeling and imitation within a social group. When a person wants to change his behavior—for example, to give up smoking—

the extent to which he can find social support for this change is critical to his success. No amount of badgering or pressure is as effective as connections with others who have gone through the same experience and successfully quit smoking.

Social learning theory provides an underpinning for groups such as Alcoholics Anonymous or Weight Watchers, where people are supported in making difficult positive changes by others who have successfully made the same changes. Workplace mentoring is another example of this approach in action. Of course, it should be acknowledged that social learning need not always be positive; less healthy behaviors can be reinforced in the same way. From the perspective of the educator, however, it represents an important dynamic that can support learning in a very powerful way.

These ideas come together in the notion of situated learning (Lave & Wenger, 1991). As discussed in the last chapter, people learn through taking part in a community of practice and gaining competence over time. The role of the educator is to encourage and support that participation using techniques such as scaffolding, whereby learners are given high levels of support initially and then less as they gain competence. To illustrate this idea, imagine that you are learning to change the oil in your car. Absolutely the best way for many of us would be to be shown on the car by somebody who knows the process well. This reflects the place (beside the car), the time (when the car needs the oil change), and the people (the more skilled mechanic). The next time the oil needs changing, you might feel capable to tackle it yourself. If that were the case, the scaffolding would have been removed, and the oil change would have moved from the zone of proximal development into your individual competency. The same structure applies to many learning contexts—piano lessons, riding a bike, cooking, and so on.

The idea of learning as a situated activity raises another issue that was less important in older views of knowledge. This is the problem of transferability. If we do indeed learn in a specific setting, to what extent can that knowledge be applied elsewhere, and how? Transfer of learning is gathering attention as situated approaches become more widely accepted as ways to conceptualize teaching and learning. I will return to issues of transferability in Chapter Nine.

When applying situated learning ideas in an educational context, there are three central implications. First, group work can be really important and powerful as a way for individuals to expand their individual knowledge and abilities, potentially further than they could have gone on their own. Second, peer tutoring—calling on the diverse experience and knowledge of adults in the class—can be far more effective than the educator teaching all the time. Learners expect their educator to be able to perform the tasks they are learning—that is why the educator has that position. But working with somebody who can successfully overcome the challenge and who is, like them, a learner, can be highly motivating. Finally, the suggestion that people learn through performing authentic tasks in specific contexts supports problem-based learning, wherein people try to figure out for themselves how to be successful. Bringing together all three of these strategies can be a very helpful way to encourage and support learning. I believe the role of the educator is to create the context for the learning to happen and then to get out of the way!

The body of evidence strongly suggests that the context experienced by the learner is an important factor in learning and cannot be ignored or expected to look after itself. In many ways, the context can be seen as the dominant factor in learning, with the educator and the learners simply part of a bigger story. To understand and shape context is to understand and shape learning.

BALL GOWN OR BOOTS: FORMALITY

The first dimension of context I will examine is formality. Despite the subheading, this is not really about the type of clothing that educators can wear to work; rather, it is about the structure of education. The European Union has gone some way toward developing a clear definition of three different levels of formality in learning:

• *Formal learning* consists of learning that occurs in an organized and structured context (formal education, in-company training) and that is designed as learning. It may lead to a formal recognition (diploma, certificate). Formal learning is intentional from the learner's perspective

• *Non-formal learning* consists of learning embedded in planned activities that are not explicitly designated as learning, but which contain an important learning element. Non-formal learning is intentional from the learner's point of view.

• *Informal learning* is defined as learning resulting from daily life activities related to work, family, or leisure. It is often referred to as experiential learning and can to a certain degree be understood as accidental learning. It is not structured in terms of learning objectives, learning time, and/or learning support.

Typically, it does not lead to certification. Informal learning may be intentional, but in most cases it is not (European Commission, 2001).

Looking across these three levels of formality, one of the obvious differences is the degree to which the learning is structured *as learning.* So in a formal context there will be intention to learn, an organized curriculum, and most likely some form of assessment. This is what most people usually think of when they picture education or learning. It looks a lot like school or university.

In this context educators must recognize certain constraints. For example, the areas of the course that can be negotiated with learners may be quite restricted because of the need to move through a certain amount of content in a certain amount of time. The existence of certification as an outcome tends to pull the class in certain directions. In its extreme form this becomes "teaching to the test," but even when it's not so blatant, assessment does influence what happens in a course.

One key point about these constraints is that they are external. They are not generated by the people within the learning context, yet those people do have to find a way to respond to them. A responsible educator will try, as much as possible, to use whatever freedom they have to work alongside learners in creating the program.

Non-formal education is where adult education has historically been strongest. Again, there is an intention to learn, but the outcome may not be related to learning. In a community setting a group of women who get together to lobby for better street lighting and more regular policing to reduce crime in their area are unlikely to describe their purpose in terms of learning, but they do have to learn about local politics in order to achieve their end. There is no certification or prescribed curriculum in this case; instead, there is a group of people coming together to do what they must. Over the last several hundred years, adult education has supported this kind of activity among factory workers, women, people struggling with literacy, marginalized ethnic groups, and union members, and in many other locations (Kelly, 1992).

The structure present in non-formal contexts tends to be created by the individuals involved in learning. They can decide how often to meet, what to talk about, and when their work is to be done. Learners can choose materials, find resources, and assess their own progress toward their goals. This process can be extremely valuable to groups and has the potential to bring about social change.

Working as an educator in such a context requires a particular set of competencies and experience, because it can be far more challenging to teach without the framework provided by externally imposed expectations.

Informal learning is the least externally structured, the most situated, and perhaps the most invisible form of learning. If somebody decides to read a book because she is interested in a topic, it is very unlikely that she will frame it as learning in any meaningful way, and certainly not as education. Informal learning occurs all the time, as part of daily social interaction, and when people say "you never stop learning" it's often this kind of learning they are talking about. It is interesting to consider the role of the educator in informal learning. There really is no role for educators, or perhaps it is better to say that there is no need for the role of educator because everybody is an educator. With no intention to learn and no external structure driving the learning (though external factors may have a general influence), there are no intermediaries of any type between the learner and the learning.

Creating courses is a concern only in formal and non-formal contexts. It should not be a surprise that in real life there is not always a clean separation between these two types of education. In both contexts learners share an intention to learn, and there is a huge variety of possible frameworks around this, ranging from the most formal school or university setting to informal book clubs or other groups of people brought together by shared interests. The challenge for educators is matching their courses to the formality of the context. The key to building this match is understanding which aspects of the context are predetermined. Are there specific learning outcomes that the educator has to aim for? Are there some materials that must be used? Is there a particular form of assessment that needs to be applied? Very often there are some framing elements present, even in the most informal settings, but significant areas of discretion and control are also available to educators.

One group of educators I am often impressed by is first aid instructors. They are teaching skills that are literally life-or-death, yet quite often they can tailor their presentations to the audience and use lots of illustrations to make their material understandable and memorable to the people in their class. In some ways their work has hallmarks of formal education, in that they must be certain that learners can perform procedures correctly, but other aspects are more reminiscent of informal settings. Their effectiveness comes, I believe, from their understanding of the limits of formality and informality in their work.

It is critical that educators pay attention to formality, especially as they engage in a new teaching context. In similar contexts with similar outcomes there may be quite different expectations regarding the formality of education, and misjudging this aspect of the context may have serious implications. When entering a new situation, it is worth explicitly asking what the key expectations and formal structures are. It is then far easier to design your teaching to recognize and accommodate those factors.

WIRED LEARNING

The issues around face-to-face, distance, and online education are currently evolving very quickly indeed. As I write this, Massive Open Online Courses (MOOCS) are being offered free of charge by some of the best universities in the world, and there is much talk of a changed educational paradigm (which happens quite a lot). In this section I would like to set aside the hype and excitement about the possibilities of online education to discuss the design issues and to what extent they are different from a face-to-face or other type of course.

As discussed in the introduction, I have chosen not to put a lot of emphasis in this book on whether a course is online or face-to-face. Although some may see this as a mistake, in my experience the way decisions have to be made (the main topic of this book) is not terribly different when some or all of the course is online. In fact, I think we are moving rapidly beyond the point where the division between face-to-face and online education will mean very much—I think almost all education will have at least some online content. I suspect that examples at either end of the continuum, either all face-to-face and no online or all online and no face-to-face, will be increasingly rare. Because of these developments, the "online or not" nature of courses is becoming less important than the conceptions behind the design and delivery of learning.

There is little doubt that online education is attaining a very high technical level. The existence of cheap broadband makes it possible for people to view television-quality video at home and to chat and complete assessments with no time lag. Some of the current tools allow for group work and whole class discussion by video and text. This assumes, of course, that learners have access to the computers and infrastructure they need. Nonetheless, it is very likely that within a few years interaction online will be approaching the richness that can be delivered in a face-to-face class.

When reviewing the literature on designing online courses (see Anderson & Elloumi, 2004; Siragusa, Dixon, & Dixon, 2007), it is striking that the design decisions are almost identical to those in any other form of education. There are some critical differences that I will discuss later, but the ways of thinking about how the course is going to work are not very different from those for courses with no online component. The same sort of criteria can be used to choose among the various options that the educator can bring to the course. For example, the way that outcomes are brought to the planning process may not vary at all from the more traditional approach, and the selection of resources will be similar (although video content will often be more practical online).

Where online education really diverges from other formats is in the methods that can be used. Some of these differences come from the technical aspects of the system that is being used. Some online systems, for example, allow easy division of learners into groups; others do not. Some have live video set up for conversations with and between different people; others do not. In the last few years, inspired by the way some social media platforms work, online learning systems have become better at linking to all sorts of diverse content in an attractive and effective way. Some differences in methods come from the nature of online learning itself, in that learners are not all in the same geographical location.

It is important for educators to understand how online and face-to-face (or other distance) modes are going to be integrated. In my experience, it can be considerably easier to develop a blended course with some face-to-face contact than one with none at all. Anecdotally, many other educators have had a similar experience. This seems to be mainly about relationships, in that meeting people face-to-face, even very briefly, provides a lot of insights into people that would take far longer to glean from online interaction. So learners can get to know each other and the educator better in far less time, providing invaluable context for online communication. If a face-to-face meeting is not possible, it is important to spend time online in introductory activities. Preferably these should go beyond sharing introductory paragraphs, to some form of activity. If appropriate, video introductions can help a lot as well. The key point to bear in mind is that if there is no face-to-face time, then all the group processes and relationship building must happen online, and space must be provided for this to take place.

A key decision in online learning is how information will be shared. This is not as pressing an issue in face-to-face settings, where instructors can talk to learners and contextualize information well, and learners can ask questions easily and quickly. If online modes of information sharing are being used, there are choices between using videos (either on YouTube or of the instructor delivering "mini-lectures"), text, readings, other websites, and so on. The stakes are higher than in face-to-face settings because it is usually harder to have a conversation about what is being taught. The media chosen have to carry more of the weight. There is no hard and fast rule about selecting media—as with so much of teaching, it has to be based on experience and feedback from learners.

The question of designing learning as an individual or group activity for online contexts must be given careful thought. The default has often been highly individual learning, with each learner going through the course essentially alone. Discussion groups can be a way to add more interaction, but often people do not contribute to them, which ends up raising the same question as does the quiet person in class: are they quiet because they are listening and learning, or are they confused and bored? Ideally, interaction should be built into the course as an essential aspect of progress, perhaps as part of assessment. It's also worth bearing in mind that learners do not have to interact within the actual course to be building relationships. It is quite likely that emails, tweets, and Facebook are being used for backchannel conversations, so even if people are not using formal discussion boards, it's likely that a lot of collaboration is occurring.

One very important dimension in online education is the availability of multi-person videoconferencing. If people can talk to each other easily in real time and can choose to move into "private" chats for working groups, online education can come much closer to the complexity of interaction that is possible face-to-face. Talking is still much faster than typing for most people, and instant feedback from another person can really help people to grasp and develop ideas.

I should offer a couple of cautions concerning online education. First, because of the way many online tools are designed, it can be difficult to create truly open frameworks with opportunities for learners to deeply influence learning. In my experience, this often makes online learning easier to design in more formal learning contexts where a set of predetermined outcomes can flow into specified content and assessment. I do not mean that informal online education is impossible, but that it takes deliberate care to avoid the formalizing tendency that seems to be inherent in many online tools.

Second, we need to remember that access to fast computers and broadband is far from universal. This certainly varies widely throughout the world, but even in affluent societies some people have the equipment to watch videos and take part in live chat, whereas others do not. As the Internet first developed, many people were concerned about the digital divide—the different experiences of the people who had the resources to benefit from the new technology and those who did not. More recently, this is mentioned less often, thanks to the widespread adoption of relatively cheap online computing, but it does have to be acknowledged in course design. This could become an issue when some learners have good experience and skills in online contexts and others may never have even used email. On the technical level, the difference between online and face-to-face components is becoming less significant, but on the social level there are still concerns to be addressed.

ORGANIZATIONAL CONTEXT

Few educators work alone. We are almost all part of a bigger organizational context, with profound implications for our work. However formal or informal organizations are, they have their own interests to serve, and this means, generally, that the educators working at that organization have to recognize the same interests. This basic idea underpins many of the rules, procedures, and expectations that we have come to recognize within our own context. Sometimes these structures can be extremely helpful; at other times they may be deeply frustrating. Whether positive or negative, these organizational factors make a huge difference to what we can teach and how.

One important aspect is the extent to which educating adults is the main purpose of the organization. Some of us work in organizations where the whole point of the organization is teaching, such as colleges, universities, school board adult education, and some community organizations. For other organizations, education can be less central, such as in a union, or even a sideline, as in a company that provides some training to employees. Either of these situations can have advantages and disadvantages depending on the details. Sometimes being part of an organization that does nothing but education means you get more resources but the programs are more centrally controlled. When it's more of a sideline, you may have to scramble for every whiteboard marker but also may have a great deal more freedom in the way you deliver teaching.

Different types of organizations have different expectations, different resources, and different structures for learning. The relationship between the adult education parts of the organization and the other parts will be different as well. In some cases, the main function of the organization (be it health care or making automobiles) will dominate very strongly, with education for adults as a support activity. In other cases, the lines may not be so clear. For example, educating trade union members about the correct grounds for grievances is not so clearly a "side" activity for a trade union, and from some perspectives could be seen as a central reason for their existence.

Every organization is driven by a set of values, and these apply as much in their educational areas as in any other. If an educator is working for a company that genuinely believes its employees are its most valuable asset, there are many opportunities to deliver wide-ranging topics in an interesting way. However, if the company believes that education has value only when it can be shown to directly increase the profit margin, the options open to the educator are likely to be far more limited.

The values relate to the management style of the organization as well. Does the organization monitor all of its employees closely (including educators) or are there opportunities to try different things? Is there a strict set of expectations that educators have to meet? Is the focus on outcomes or on activity? Is your course likely to be canceled if you don't reach a certain number of participants? Although many of the examples I've given here are from more formal settings, the same kinds of questions should be asked about informal, community-based education, where there will still be expectations and perhaps even more important values to be recognized.

The expectations do not always come from the organization alone, as they themselves may have responsibilities to wider society that have to be recognized. One of the most pressing for many organizations is the need to report their activities to a funder and to fit with the plan the funder has paid them to follow. In some of the more extreme cases, the organization can end up devoting almost as much time to reporting on its programs as it does to delivering them. This type of external requirement takes great care to handle and can be frustrating for the educator. Any educator can find herself in a position in which her experience and knowledge of education are undervalued, with teaching seen as a neutral activity that can be bent to fit any requirement. The position throughout this book is that this is not the case, and that the context, the learners, and who you are as an educator matter a great deal.

The complexity of organizational context can sometimes be difficult for educators to deal with. The most useful approach to these factors, in my view, is to consider negotiation as part of your role as an educator. In other words, there are a range of people with different interests surrounding a program, and part of your role as educator is to ensure that you do not lose sight of the interests of the people closest to the programs—educators and learners. Even though the knowledge we possess as educators is not always acknowledged, our experience and our position in the organization allow us to develop unique and valuable insights into the design and delivery of education.

The idea of negotiation as part of the educator's job is based on a highly influential study of the program planning process (Cervero & Wilson, 1994). The authors talk about the negotiation of interests, which they define as "motivations and purposes that lead people to act in certain ways" (p. 29), as a meeting of rationality and politics. On one side lie the actions and decisions that the educator judges are necessary and useful to make programs effective. On the other side are the actions and decisions that reflect the experience of working within a particular organization; for example, subjects that have to be included in the program to ensure it is funded. Although it is easy to dismiss these as irrelevant annoyances that make it harder to develop programs, it is important to remember that dealing with these factors is what makes programs possible at all. The aim is not to promote one set of interests, whether rational or political, at the expense of the other, but to reach some kind of accommodation and balance.

The term negotiation, in this case, has two meanings. One is the more common meaning of discussing ideas with people who may see things differently, the aim being to reach some sort of agreement on the best course of action. The second meaning is working with the interests of all involved in a facilitative role. Educators must not only promote what they consider the best way to do things but also take into account what others expect and need from the program (Cervero & Wilson, 1994). Another approach is to view your responsibility as an educator as being to teach the best class that is possible within the context. It won't always be the ideal class, but our role as educators is to deliver the most effective education we can given the specific circumstances of our work.

The organization they work within may be a strong or a less strong fit for educators and their values. However good the fit, they will still need to take certain aspects into account in designing courses, and however difficult this may be, there is usually a way for educators to shape the teaching in ways that they see as important. The key, as in so many aspects of course design, is to be aware of these structural dimensions and respond to them thoughtfully and responsibly in planning.

THE AIMS OF THE COURSE

Although there are lots of external factors that make a difference to the way you can teach in any given course, there are also features of the course itself that will have an influence. Every class is not going to be the same—after all, it would be a bit odd if poets and doctors learned their crafts in the same way. (There would be a worrying number of rather clinical poems and highly imaginative metaphorical diagnoses.) What the class is trying to achieve will have quite a strong influence on the process followed and the outcomes aimed for. Of course, it is probably worth adding that the relationship between topic and process is not quite as clear-cut as it once was.

One of the most important internal factors to consider in designing a course is the topic. Some topics require a different type of treatment from others. To illustrate this, we can look at two very different topics, biology and politics. Learning biology involves a high level of focus on facts about the natural world, naming systems, chemistry of plants, and so on. Learning politics—say, the history of recent U.S. presidents—has a different set of requirements. Here there are identifiable facts that are useful to know, such as the date of President Kennedy's assassination or who started the New Deal, but the emphasis of the course lies much more strongly on making sense of political decisions and analyzing the alternatives. This plays out in the teaching methods and the assessment approaches, which have to cover both the factual content and the analytical skills that are not easily reduced to simple statements of competencies.

Traditionally, there has been a view that the learning of facts and the application of analytical skills were really two quite distinct types of activity, seen as happening not only in different topics but also in different stages of learning the topics. A good example of this can be found in learning languages, where the traditional assumption was that new speakers of French had to learn all the verb tables and tenses before they could learn to speak the language and use it in everyday circumstances. Over the last few years this really rigid distinction has come to be seen as less than useful. Current thinking is that whenever possible knowledge of facts and the ability to analyze can be developed together.

To take a concrete example, trades education is an area of specialization for many people educating adults. The outcome of this education is necessarily practical—people have to learn to build a wall if they are going to be masons. However, the course cannot just be about lining up bricks. The pragmatic art of masonry involves a lot of thought and planning. Calculations have to be made, and site and materials considered. It takes a lot of thought and knowledge to build a wall, much of it very similar to what we would call theory in another context. This is true in every case I can think of—concrete practices and the meaning of those practices are embedded in each other.

If this idea is accepted as a principle of design, then the way that educators think about their courses is quite different. Instead of thinking about whether the course we are teaching has a focus on facts or a focus on analysis, we must consider where the balance lies and how learners can develop these different aspects together. Educators do not always have complete control over the content of courses or the outcomes. One obvious case is safety training, for which the curriculum is laid out in a great deal of detail and mastery of the content is imperative. Here there is little room for negotiation of the outcomes or, often, of the teaching process itself. There may be videos that must be watched and set procedures that must be followed. This is an extreme example, but even here there is the possibility for building exercises that pull together practical actions and the understanding that lies behind them. One example of this kind of activity is scenarios, which allow learners to work through a range of situations and possible solutions.

It is the educator's role to design a course that makes sense, given the intended aims and the various people involved—especially given the interests of the learners. There is no one way to teach each subject. As an educator you have both the responsibility and the power to decide the types of abilities that the course will help to develop. This will vary depending on a number of factors but will represent a balance of pragmatic and analytical intentions. The role of the educator is finding this balance. If we do our job well, we can create situations where learners are totally focused on a relevant, hands-on activity that also helps them to analyze situations in a more profound way. This can be a powerful experience for the learners and the educator.

TIME, OR THE LACK THEREOF

In this and the following section I will touch on the use of resources that are available in the context of your work. Of all the available resources, the hardest to work around is time. For the educator, there is contact time, spent in the presence of learners, and non-contact time, usually spent on preparation and assessment. In some contexts, the educators are paid for ample contact time and sufficient non-contact time, and they have the opportunity to create really interesting teaching structures. In my experience, this is not the usual situation. More commonly, especially for part-time educators, contact time is credited, but non-contact time is invisible. Sometimes it can look like you are getting well paid for your work as an educator until the non-contact time is taken into account. Depending on the educator's experience and the type of course, the ratio of non-contact time to contact time may be low; for example, half an hour for every hour of in-class teaching. However, the other extreme—with three hours or more of non-contact time for every hour of contact time—is not uncommon. I would estimate that in my university teaching I probably have a ratio of about five to one when marking is taken into account. If I was getting $30 an hour for my teaching, which at first glance looks pretty healthy, I would be making less than minimum wage when all the real time was taken into account.

This is not about educators being greedy about pay. It is about the limited number of hours in a week and the need to do a good job of teaching and still have time to do whatever else needs to be done to earn a living. When planning a course, it's important to think through the non-contact time and work out how much can realistically be dedicated to the program. The more structured the class, the more non-contact time you need. More formal assessment requires more time. If you have more people in the course, it will typically take more time for feedback and general learning support. Sometimes this varies over the course of a class, with more time available at certain points and less at others. It's a good idea to budget time carefully, both for the contact and the non-contact hours.

Learners' time also matters. Sometimes learners can devote many hours to the class both in and outside the classroom, but often they can't. Homework is a standard part of the Western learning culture, but it's also quite a strange idea when you think about it. If we were at work and put in our eight-hour day and then were asked to do more at home, we'd certainly notice (though we might choose to do it anyway, for all sorts of reasons). But the time learners invest outside contact hours is once more considered to be basically invisible. This is becoming more and more of a challenge in certain contexts, such as programs for working people. This is a very different group of learners from the traditional undergraduates, as their time is at even more of a premium. They have families and full-time jobs, and if you ask them to read something, you better have a darn good reason. This can be good for teaching, introducing a high level of discipline around what people are asked to do at home. By all means educators should ask people to do some work at home, but it's important that it is purposeful and carefully selected.

When meeting with learners, it is a good rule of thumb that there is *never* enough time. Educators are responsible for managing time actively and ensuring that it is well used. Letting activities and conversations reach a natural end is usually not an option, so it's as well to have your best guess at time allocations for different sections of the course written down in advance and then try to stick to it. Of course, you also have to use your judgment. If a specific item really catches fire and people want to stick with it, then it's good to have an extra few minutes up your sleeve. For a two-hour literacy class, a schedule could look something like:

10–10:15	Reflections and questions from last week
10:15–10:45	Discussion of "found" literacy examples (bills, flyers, letters, and so on)
10:45–11:00	New vocabulary
11:00–11:15	Coffee and cookie break
11:15–11:45	Small group reading exercises
11:45–12:00	Review and wind up

Even though I've been teaching adults for quite a while, I still do a plan like this for *every* class. Note the review and wind-up time. Fifteen minutes is too long for this. The reason it's longer is that it will provide buffer time to cover the way that other sections will overrun, nearly every time.

In summary, there are two points when considering time. The first is to try to make the invisible time visible and take it into account, whether it is the educator's time or the learners'. The extra hours matter. The second point is simply to use time well. More time does not equal more learning unless it is used in carefully crafted ways.

SOMEWHERE TO SIT: PHYSICAL RESOURCES

The context educators are working in makes a difference to the physical resources that are available.

Many a brilliant and potentially effective plan for teaching falls apart because of a mismatch between the resources available and what is needed, so when creating courses it makes sense to think carefully about resources, to avoid possible frustration. Either the resources that are needed can be found in advance or the teaching plan can be designed to match what is available. It is of course true that resources by themselves do not improve teaching or learning. An uninteresting course will not be improved by adding tons of resources. But thoughtful and imaginative use of the available resources can be a great asset to your teaching.

The physical setting for teaching and learning matters a lot (except for online courses, where everybody can be at home in their pajamas and nobody is any the wiser). First of all, there is a question of comfort. It used to be common for adults to be taught in elementary schools, until somebody finally realized that asking full-size people to sit in those tiny chairs wasn't really a great idea. The space you are using needs to be welcoming and quite quiet. Acoustics matter here—a space that is too echoey can make it hard to hear across the group. One of the great challenges of educating adults almost everywhere in the world is temperature. A room that is too cold or too hot will stall learning in its tracks, so having control of the thermostat can be critical. Seating distribution makes a big difference; ideally it should be designed to be flexible so that people can cluster or spread out depending on the demands of the activity.

Even though we live in an allegedly wired age, it's really helpful to have something in the room to write on. This can be a whiteboard or flip chart (though then you always need to remember to have the right pens) or a chalkboard. If you are having small groups discuss an idea and then share their ideas with the whole class, being able to give each group something big to write on can make the reporting back more interesting, especially if you ask participants to draw pictures rather than write bullet points.

At this point, I would like to insert a note about the resources that are perhaps closest to my own heart—food and drink. Having snacks and coffee, tea, or water matters a great deal. It's become common sense that children learn better in school when they have eaten breakfast. Adults are not too different in this regard. It's hard to concentrate on anything when you are hungry. In addition, sharing food and drink is a positive and group-building experience in most cultures in the world, so there are powerful emotional benefits. One of my favorite things is for people to bring food they have selected or made to each class meeting so that everybody can get some insight into the learners' home culture. There are times when this isn't appropriate (it's really hard to get people to share haggis), but where it can be done, it can help build great rapport.

Technology is an amazing aid to teaching, and I really enjoy working in a classroom with a data projector and access to the Internet. There are huge numbers of incredibly useful resources out there, and it can help make the class more interesting for people to be able to watch a video or look at a photograph together. However, any technology, just like resources more generally, needs to be used wisely. One of the greatest teaching mistakes over the past fifteen years has been overuse of presentation software to present endless slideshows. There is quite a lot of information out there on how to do it well, but unfortunately not too many people seem to pay attention to it. Presentation software is at its best when used to show images, and at its worst when it presents endless text. I've reached the point where if I need to present a mini-lecture I will make up a slideshow and then print it out and give it to folks. It's still a bit dull, but at least I can keep the lights on and people get to make notes without having to copy down the slide contents.

Related to technology, but much more traditional, is the question of access to materials. Sometimes the educator has a library of materials including a curriculum and all the books, videos, and other supports needed to deliver it. More often, I suspect, educators working with adults have a range of supplies that are sort of appropriate but need to be organized and supplemented in lots of ways. For some classes it can be surprising how little you actually need in order to do a great job, but for others access to materials is vital. Learning a language would be really hard, for example, without dictionaries and materials to work with.

Some of the materials for adult learning are really good, but others present more of a challenge. For years one of the concerns of literacy instructors has been that the materials available for introductory learners have been really more appropriate for children than for adults. In response to this, literacy instructors in different parts of the world have produced their own materials. This can be a really valuable option, as the materials can reflect the class more closely than anything produced elsewhere and can follow the interests of the learners. Another advantage of educators compiling their own materials is that they can be photocopied and distributed more widely without concerns about copyright.

A final area of concern is the educator-to-learner ratio. It may seem odd to consider this in a resources section, but it influences not only how much time each learner can reasonably expect to be devoted to them but also what sort of teaching strategies make sense. With six learners, individual presentations to the group can be interesting and helpful. With thirty this is not such a viable strategy. It's much easier with a smaller group to follow their interests, either individually or together. The presence and significance of the educator is going to be different in groups of different sizes. In my experience, working with smaller groups is energizing—the educator finishes the allotted time feeling motivated and engaged. With larger groups, the educator can be exhausted by the end of the class time unless there is a clear agenda and careful plan to follow. In larger groups a lot of time is spent in what schoolteachers call classroom management. These are the tasks involved in putting people into groups, mixing people around (if desired), getting people's reactions to the tasks and ensuring they are motivated, and so on. This can be done a lot more directly and quickly in a smaller group. When thinking through a plan for a class, it is helpful to acknowledge these differences and make sure they are being considered in your design.

This section really underlines the extent to which education is a pragmatic, concrete business. Ideas and values are absolutely critical, but there are some fundamental aspects of working with adults in a teaching situation that cannot be ignored. The time you have, the number of students, the location of the class, the teaching tools that are available make a huge difference. No particular setup is necessarily better than any other; your role as an educator is to work well with what is available. When you are designing a course it is critical to know what you have to work with. The situation you want to avoid is walking into a room full of people with three hours' worth of brilliance on a memory stick—only to discover there is no computer!

Surprisingly, the type of organization you are working with, and the centrality of education to their activities, is no guarantee of the amount and quality of the available resources. Community groups do not necessarily have only simple resources while universities the best and brightest—it is always important to clarify what you can expect when you arrive to teach.

CONCLUSION

This chapter has discussed a broad range of contextual factors and how they might affect the work done by educators. Going beyond the specifics of all of these discussions is, I think, a very pressing question for educators: how much should they fit their work to the context and how much should they try to change the context? There is, of course, no "one size fits all" answer to this question. For some educators their ability to work to a certain set of values outweighs any other consideration, and for these folks it is really important to find a context that suits and supports them. Others do not really have a strong philosophical position and are happy to be extremely flexible in their approach. Most people fall somewhere in between: willing to work with many cultural constraints but with a clear idea of what is not acceptable. As with so many other aspects of education, for adults or otherwise, balance matters a great deal.

For people who are new to educating adults, I believe there is a strong case for really understanding the context well and making informed and thoughtful decisions. Very often the constraints are really not as solid as they might appear. I remember working with an agency that had a strong historical commitment to the labor movement. The education delivered by this agency avoided mentioning unions, and indeed, the educators went to great lengths to ensure this didn't happen. As part of my work there, I got to know the funders of the programs, and asked them why they didn't want unions mentioned. They replied that they did—in fact, that was the whole point of funding this particular agency to deliver the programs. The agency, and the educators within it, were seeing a contextual barrier that, as it turned out, did not exist.

Responding well to context is one of the central arts of the educator of adults. There is no shortcut to developing the sort of practical wisdom that it takes to do this, but by acknowledging contextual factors and thinking carefully about their influence on your educational practice, you are already well on your way to developing it.

PART TWO

The Key Decisions

The first part of the book looked at contextual factors that affect how courses for adults are designed. The second part is more concrete; it focuses on six areas in which the course designer needs to make choices. Throughout this part there is no attempt to tell you what you should decide. Instead, my aim is to help you understand the implications of whatever decisions you make.

There is a chapter for each of the six areas, which we can call *design elements* in keeping with the theme of the book. They are:

- *Aims.* This chapter discusses what sorts of objectives are needed in the creation of a course and how they can be developed.

- *Resources for learning.* There are important decisions to be made about the actual information that will be involved in the course, and what will most effectively support it.

- *Methods.* This refers to the ways in which the educator will actually teach and the role of the learners in the course.

- *Learner input.* Students should be involved in making design decisions and should have opportunities to provide feedback on the course as a whole. This chapter discusses how to ensure this.

- *Demonstrating learning.* There are a range of ways to assess and demonstrate learning, if this is necessary. This chapter looks at some of the considerations that come into play when the educator is choosing how to assess.

- *Transfer of learning.* For many educators, it is important to know how learners will use what they have learned after they leave the course and how teaching can make it more likely that the knowledge will be both useful and used.

I have selected these six design elements because they are inclusive of the most important elements of teaching and learning as I have come to know them. Other divisions were possible, but I think that the approach here is relatively simple and logically organized. It would be silly to suggest that people design courses by working through each area in turn, but it can be helpful when thinking about design to have some sort of framework to work from. It is important to acknowledge that the six design elements are not entirely independent; choices in one area will affect the other elements. More than this, a common philosophy or set of values may tend to push the six elements in the same direction, as might a particular group of learners or context. The aim is not to deny this interconnectedness, but rather to make sure the design of the course is visible and decisions are being taken deliberately.

The chapters on the design elements have been designed to include three aspects:

- Each of the chapters has sections on the contextual factors from the first part of the book so that the effects of the educator, the learners, and the context can be discussed and their implications explored. This organization makes it easy to find the sections you would like to read to reflect a specific decision you have to make. If, for example, you need to think about the way that the educational experiences of the learners might affect assessment it is simple to find that specific section.

- Each chapter starts with a brief vignette, and this example is used throughout the chapter, to provide consistency to the chapters and allow for deeper exploration of particular situations that often face educators.

- There is a set of guiding questions for each design element, intended to help you to think through the design options open to you. In the last part of each chapter I summarize the way each question has been approached.

In the final chapter of this section I pull together all the previous discussion into a single overarching framework. This cannot replace the discussion throughout the book, but it should help to pull together the wide-ranging topics covered into a coherent and concrete approach.

I have tried to provide pointers to different and, I hope, useful ways to think about all the various aspects of course design, but in the end you, as the educator, will need to make the key decisions. Working through these chapters will not replace the need for you to design a course that you are comfortable with on every level. I hope that they may, however, provide some support in that process.

chapter FOUR

Knowing Where You Are Going

AIMS

Who has power to identify aims?

How do resources affect aims?

What aims are not viable?

Are objectives necessary?

How specific?

Who are the objectives for?

Solange has worked for NGOs for eight years, usually as an administrator. She loves the environment and the working context, as well as the opportunity to work for something she believes in rather than just a paycheck. She previously worked for an organization supporting people with mental health issues and for an agency that provided job training to unemployed people, and now she is happy to be part of an environmental group, Cheminvert. The aim of the organization is to work for change toward sustainability at both the global and the local level. This means that they are interested in working with the local council to encourage recycling as well as advocating nationally on behalf of strategies to slow down climate change.

Solange now finds herself in a position of some responsibility in the educational area of the organization. Cheminvert prepares and distributes educational resources for schoolchildren, offers in-depth workshops on environmental issues for adults, goes into businesses to inform them about sustainable options, and has a public education role through brochures, online video, and whatever media attention they can garner. This strikes Solange as a lot of activity, all pointing in different directions and requiring different strategies.

The executive director has asked Solange to act as the director of public education. As Cheminvert is a relatively small agency, this means she will be planning and delivering all the educational outreach activities. She is thrilled to take on more of a frontline role in the organization and is determined to do a good job. Early in her new position, she heard from the executive director that the board of the organization had some doubts about the educational activities of the organization, and he underlined how important it is that Solange be clear about what she wants to achieve.

After talking to some other educators in different contexts, Solange knows that one way she can address this question is by developing really clear objectives for the educational activities. However, not only is she unsure how best to go about this on a general level, but she also doesn't have much experience setting objectives for individual courses and workshops. Her predecessor hasn't been much help. He tended to believe that any way of getting the message out was a good thing, even though this approach ended up costing Cheminvert a lot of money and time. His argument was always that being too "linear" could alienate some of the people who might end up helping with the work of the agency, and Solange can see some merit in this argument.

Her immediate challenge is how to manage her first workshop, coming up in about two weeks. It is for a group of people who live in an apartment building in a less privileged part of the city. Many of their children have heard about the environment at school, and the residents want to respond to their children's concerns by finding ways to put more sustainable practices into place in the apartment block. Solange knows this is a really important opportunity for Cheminvert, perhaps even leading to a demonstration project, and she is keen to go into it with a clear agenda.

It seems like common sense that the first thing you need to know when you start designing a course is the aim you want to achieve. After all, if you aren't sure where you are going, how can you know which direction to head in and when you've arrived? The most common way to think about these questions is to consider the objectives of the course. Quite a few different words are commonly used to express the same idea as "objective"—words such as "outcome," "goal," "aim"— but in educational design, objectives generally have a very specific meaning: they are detailed statements of what people should learn by participating in the program. An example would be "by the end of this course, you will be able to weld two tubes of mild steel together without distortion or leaks" or "participants will be able to summarize the five main reasons for the end of the Roman Empire." For a number of reasons, which will be discussed in the next section, the idea of objectives is very appealing.

Unfortunately, objectives are not quite as simple as they appear. They are not self-evident, but the product of a lot of thinking and planning. In some cases, using objectives to plan the course may not be at all appropriate; they could even get in the way of what the instructor and the learners are trying to achieve. Some people are very skeptical about objectives and see them as far more harmful to learning than helpful.

If we are going to use objectives, and use them well, it's important to know what the options are and the sorts of uses objectives can be put to. In this chapter, I will cover the following questions about the general intended effects of the course and objectives in particular:

- Who has the power to decide what the aims of the course should be?
- How do the available resources affect the aims?
- Are there certain types of aims that cannot be brought about by this course?
- Are detailed objectives for learning necessary?
- How specific do objectives for learning need to be?
- To whom are the objectives intended to communicate?

In starting this discussion, there is one point to bear in mind. Because objectives provide a detailed roadmap for the course, different courses with the same intended aims could easily have different detailed objectives. For example, you may be putting together a course to help employees learn a new accounting software package. The objectives would not be the same for a group of new employees as for a group of established employees who were familiar with the old package. In the case of the experienced group, you might have as an objective something like "identify the changed procedures for posting an expense claim," because they know the overall framework. For new employees, the objective might be "become familiar with our company's processes for posting claims." The main thing to bear in mind is that there are lots of ways of setting up objectives to achieve a certain effect, and as the educator, you can and must decide whether you are going to use objectives and, if you are, how they should be developed, and what they should be. This chapter suggests ways to make an informed decision.

OBJECTIVES—AND SOME OBJECTIONS

The idea that education should have explicit objectives has become uncontroversial in the last few years. After all, who wouldn't want a clear target to aim for? Objectives allow for evaluation of the course to be tied more closely to expectations, and objectives also give learners a far clearer idea of what they will get out of a course. Because they bring so much transparency and coherence to learning, they can very easily be seen as a clearly, commonsensically good thing. In fact, the whole discussion of objectives can be so powerful that it becomes really hard to imagine alternative ways to organize a course of learning. Is it even possible to have a course without a set of predetermined objectives that everybody knows about at the beginning?

The notion that well-defined objectives are the key to a good educational program is a relatively recent one. One of the most influential contributions to the development of objective-based education was written by Tyler (1949). He presented a very clear idea of educational objectives, based on the behaviorist philosophies that were gaining ground at the time. As discussed in Chapter Two, behaviorism claims that the whole point of education is changed behavior, interpreted broadly to include thinking and feeling as well as observable actions. If you accept this perspective, it's easy to work backward to see the whole of the educational experience as leading to that change in behavior. How the educator and the learners work together from the very start of the class should be orientated toward a particular behavioral effect.

Tyler's approach to objectives will seem familiar to people who have worked with the objective-based systems that are currently popular. He believed that an objective should have two components: the kind of behavior desired and the area of life to which it should apply. One of his examples is "to write clear and well-organized reports of social studies projects" (Tyler, 1949, p. 47). He also thought that assessment should be linked to the objectives, which makes a lot of sense. He argued that "it is very necessary to check each proposed evaluation device against the objectives that are being aimed at and to see whether it uses situations likely to evoke the sort of behavior which is desired as educational objectives" (p. 113). Putting this into practice would lead to a highly systematic way of thinking through (1) the desired behavioral change, (2) how learners could be encouraged to make that change, and (3) how their behavior could be assessed in terms of that change.

In recent years Tyler's ideas have been developed a great deal, to the point where the evaluation of learning is pretty much expected to follow directly from the objective. Objective-based education has been spreading through different parts of the education system for several decades, and there are few contexts in which it is not the dominant approach to planning courses and programs. One of the settings where objectives have found less acceptance is in university education, but this is changing rapidly. Led by European universities, higher education everywhere is creating systems of generic and discipline-specific objectives (often called learning outcomes, in this case) (Tamburri, 2013).

What we know from all of the work on developing the idea of objectives is that they get their power from their precision—the more accurate they are, the more useful they are. Objectives are a communicative device, designed to tell learners what they can expect and giving direction on the behaviors on which people will be assessed. It also can help learners to select a course if they can review the objectives and see which fit best with their intentions.

There are many resources available, on the Internet and elsewhere, that provide information on objectives: how they can best be written, what they should include, and so on. I do not want to repeat that information here; suffice to say, it's important that objectives are as specific as possible and testable. That is, you should be able to tell whether somebody has reached those objectives or not—and just as important, so should they. When it comes to objectives, "learners will understand French better" is a rather vague statement, and really not an objective at all. Expressed as an objective, this would read something like "by the end of this course the learner will be able to conjugate the six main irregular French verbs in speech and writing." It's relatively simple to see how this could be assessed and learner progress demonstrated.

SOME GOOD AND BAD OBJECTIVES FOR SOLANGE

You will know more about the environment.

This is very vague indeed and does not help either the educator or the learners know where they are going or how they will know when they get there.

You will be able to cite the five main scientific reasons that algal bloom is detrimental for sulfur dioxide dilution in nontropical sea water.

This is specific but does not sound very realistic for a public education project, or very interesting. How will Solange check that it's been achieved?

Students will be able to name the five most endangered species in North America by the end of the day.

This is a decent objective, though a little trivial. How will she check? More worrying, what will learners do with this knowledge? It would be good to have a practical outcome here. Finally, avoid using "students" with adults unless they are in formal education; even then, it should be avoided.

This workshop will provide participants with increased confidence in their ability to select sustainable everyday practices.

This is quite a good objective. Confidence could be measured with an end-of-course survey, and the application of the knowledge is very clear.

At the end of this course students will be able to demonstrate capability in analyzing their place of work for environmental hazards and recommend good practices.

This is a good objective, though quite formal for public education. Nonetheless, the time, the application, and the effect are all very clear.

A simple process to review objectives that you are writing is to ask whether somebody reading the objective, but knowing nothing about the course or the topic, could tell:

Who will be able to do *what* by *when* and *how* they can demonstrate their ability.

When objectives are being set, we must consider whether they should be the same for all the learners. Although typically they are set at the course level, making them identical for everybody, there is no reason not to set objectives for each participant. This approach has gained ground in fields such as literacy education, where all the learners have different starting points and may want different things out of the course, and it leads to "individual learning plans" and "individual learning outcomes." Setting individual objectives has many of the advantages of an objective-based approach—in that expectations can be clear for instructors and learners—and also many advantages of a more open approach, in that it encourages conversations about learning plans between educators and learners. The *disadvantage* of a highly individualized approach for the educator is that it does not help with planning the course before it starts (as you need the learners to be there to make the plans) and it can lead to much more work in assessing learning (as there must be an assessment for each of the varied objectives).

A further question is whether the objectives are going to be content specific or more general. There is a difference between the objective of "restore a Victorian oak table top" and one of "identify and use the correct cleaning product for antique wooden furniture." The difference is in the transferability—the first version is limited to a particular situation, whereas the second applies in a range of settings. Another, slightly more subtle difference is that the first is simply about doing something, whereas the second has more of a cognitive aspect because the learners demonstrating this objective have to think about what they are going to do and make informed decisions.

This more transferable type of objective is often referred to as a competency, as used in professional training programs. Canadian pharmacists, for example, have to demonstrate a range of competencies including "manage the drug distribution system to ensure the safety, accuracy and quality of supplied products" (National Association of Pharmacy Regulatory Authorities, 2007, p. 6). In a situation where educators are working toward a competency framework, as is increasingly the case, it is relatively straightforward to build course objectives around those competencies. If there is no competency framework, the educator should try to strike a balance between tightly defined, specific objectives and more transferable and potentially more analytical objectives.

For people who have fully integrated objectives or learning outcomes into their work, assessment of the course will be tightly linked to them. Some educators will deliberately not assess anything not covered by the learning outcomes, such as attendance. Others will not suggest class activities that do not relate to the outcomes. In some circumstances this way of working brings useful discipline to the course; in others, it turns out to be too deliberate and rather artificial. If the setting is appropriate, it can be very helpful to have outcomes and assessment strongly linked—again, to ensure the highest possible level of transparency and clarity. This does not require the educator to set the objectives in advance, and I strongly advocate negotiation between learners and instructors regarding what the objectives should be and how they can be assessed if necessary.

At this point, I want to step back from the discussion of objectives and ask whether they are always necessary or desirable, and what some other options might be. Before discussing the alternatives, it may be useful to summarize the potential value of objectives in planning programs. They not only help communication of the direction of the course—they actually *constitute* that direction. Indeed, many course and program planners start with the objectives and work backward to think through the evaluation, the process, and the content of the course. Objectives can act as an important foundation, anchor, and starting point for the course. Used thoughtfully and appropriately, they can really help with making the idea of a course into a concrete plan.

One big concern with using explicit objectives in the education of adults is that things are not always as logical and linear as objectives may make them appear. One response is to suggest that the various aspects of the course have to develop together, with each affecting the other and the social context also affecting the design (Caffarella, 2002). For most educators in most situations, this is probably a more accurate way of thinking about their work than trying to start from objectives and design a logically consistent course. Building too mechanically from objectives can lead to a course that is driven artificially by objectives and that does not really reflect the process as it is experienced by the educator and the participants.

There is also the possibility that overly defined objectives could get in the way of what the course is trying to achieve. Perhaps the aim of the program is to provide a space for local people to set priorities for community development; in this situation, overly defined objectives could close down the discussion. Objectives tend to assume that the educator has a relatively clear idea of the end point of the course, and this does not necessarily encourage people to feel that they can participate in an open process.

It is almost always possible to write objectives for a course, but depending on the specific course, they can end up so broad that they no longer really work as objectives in the formal sense. The aspect that often gets lost as objectives become broader is the ability to assess them easily and clearly. If the aim of the course is to support creative writing, the objective might be something like "raise people's satisfaction with their ability to express their ideas in prose." This might well be a very valuable outcome, but it is a very difficult one to demonstrate clearly.

If an educator is working on a topic, or with learners, where objectives would not work very well, there are a range of options. One is to emphasize the process of the course rather than the outcomes. This is often a useful approach when seeking high levels of participation. Instead of using tight objectives that imply a specific way of moving through the course, the course can be described primarily through the approach taken, such as "a discussion group around issues of class in American society and the individual's experience of class issues." The Scandinavian Study Circles are an outstanding example of learner-centered adult education in the world. They are based on a method of popular education wherein people come together to study issues on a very informal basis using this exact approach (Larsson & Norvall, 2010).

Another option is to focus on the theme or subject of the course, allowing it to range within that area based on the experience and interests of learners. So, for example, it would be possible to offer a course on environmental issues where the objectives were left open but the focus always remained on sustainability. This approach is used surprisingly often in professional development, where there is a defined set of topics that people need to know about but the training is driven by the interests and questions of participants. Arrangements like this can help when there is a range of people with different levels of experience.

One of the most important variations is adopting a problem-based approach: the focus of the course is the ability to diagnose and solve problems (it is often used in medical education), and the final objectives tend to reflect the problems confronting the participants. One benefit of this kind of structure is that people may be able to bring real-life problems that they are facing—for example, in their work—and find solutions in a supportive environment.

Objectives can be really important and useful in designing a course, and they should be considered by the educator. But they certainly do not automatically solve all possible issues that might arise. The options discussed here, as well as others, can offer more appropriate ways to communicate with learners about the intentions of the course and allow for more negotiations around the process. In the next three sections, I discuss what sort of considerations it can be useful to think about in making decisions about objectives.

THE EDUCATOR

If you do use objectives, many aspects of your position as an educator will affect the way you use them. One key consideration is your philosophy as an educator, which may put more emphasis on the educator's responsibility to lead the learners through their learning or on the importance of providing spaces for learners to shape their own program. This judgment will be influenced by a range of considerations such as topic, context, and audience.

Ensuring a match between your philosophy and your approach to course design is essential, but do not exclude the possibility of some degree of flexibility. It is not a comfortable situation to have built a course around a set of objectives that you thought would be appropriate, only to find that the course goes somewhere quite different (albeit even more valuable). Is it better to backtrack and come up with amended objectives that follow the evolution of the course, or try to bring it back "on track"? My own experience suggests that it is important not to fight too hard against the organic development of a course, and I do try to leave some space within objectives for these developments. I believe that shaping the course as it goes along can make for a much better course than I could dream up on my own!

Even if you are strongly committed to the concept that learners should shape the course, that does not mean you should not use objectives at all. You could enter into a collective process with the learners of defining and noting objectives and the associated assessments, if there are any. Commitment to negotiated objectives can often be really high, and adults tend to value the opportunity to participate in the planning. Also, some educators who are strongly committed to learner empowerment believe in clear objectives because they can act as a sort of "contract" for the course, creating both clarity and expectations to which learners can hold the educator.

Sometimes there is reason to value closure on the key questions of the course, and having carefully thought-through objectives can help with this. Complete clarity about the anticipated shape of the course can have great pragmatic value;

for example, if two or three people are teaching versions of the same course to learners who will then move together into a further course. In such a situation, consistency will be important enough to justify aligning objectives—and most likely any assessments—across all the different courses.

It can also be useful to have objectives if you are new to teaching a particular area or topic. In the real lives of educators, we often have to teach things for the first time, and even if we are world experts on the topic, organizing that knowledge so that it can help others to learn can be a significant challenge. The framework offered by objectives can suggest what sort of assessments could be used, how the class can be organized to get to the desired end point, and what sort of content could be included. The planning benefits of an objective-based approach should not be overlooked.

Despite the potential benefits of objectives, it is important to acknowledge that some educators find them simply objectionable for teaching adults. The origin of objectives in behaviorist psychology, with its explicit aim to change the behavior of learners, is seen as a problem. Objective-based design can be seen in this way, and perhaps even more so in recent years with the expansion of competency-centered education. There are legitimate questions about the extent to which tightly defined learning objectives can seem to deemphasize the humanity of the learners and make them sound a little like programmable learning machines. This way of relating to learners runs directly counter to the sociocultural approach and the historical precedents discussed earlier in this book.

There are similar concerns about the power implications of objectives, because if they are defined in advance it suggests that the educator has the right and the ability to decide what should be learned without the learners being involved. Because many educators working with adults are uncomfortable with being in this position, it follows that they can be reluctant to use a strongly objective-based approach.

I believe that the key is to keep the communicative function of objectives in mind when deciding whether to use objectives and how they should be shaped. If the educator can let people know what is expected of them without formal objectives (perhaps using one of the other approaches discussed in the previous section), then it seems to me there are very effective options. The educator and the learners must feel comfortable with the objectives that are set and what they communicate about the course.

In our initial vignette, Solange was quite comfortable with the idea of objectives; in fact, it appears that the lack of clear objectives was a major issue in the past. Her analysis is grounded in a belief in the usefulness of objectives as a communicative tool. Now Solange must work out what kind of communication will work for the learners and the context in which she is working.

THE LEARNERS

For learners, the most important benefits of having clear objectives are clarity and predictability. People have usually gone through a school system marked by a systematic way of doing things, with expectations set out well in advance. Marks are important to many people, and they may feel that they have been educated over many years to get good marks by responding to specific requirements. If this structure is not in place, they may feel disoriented and even fear that they will be ambushed at the end of the course with a set of expectations that they have not been prepared for.

Recently I taught a course on adult education in a university. In adult education, the independence and self-directedness of students are obviously seen as important values, but universities have very high levels of structure. There was an obvious contradiction between what was being taught and how it was being taught, and I wanted to experiment. So I set the class up as an entirely exploratory course where students would define what the course would cover and how they would demonstrate their learning.

One big challenge was that I could not take part in the discussions for setting up the course. Whatever we educators say tends to be given a great deal of weight, even when we are just musing out loud. Yet I felt I had to be there to show support and so the students could feel they had a safety net if they went in a really strange direction. I kept quiet as much as possible, and people learned that I would not offer advice or answer direct questions (I wasn't rude—I didn't ignore people!).

From this experience, which was as far from an educator-directed, objective-driven course as I could manage in a university setting, I learned an incredible amount. The first thing was how angry students got that their normal objective framework wasn't in place. It was clear that this was a source of security for the learners and that without it they felt very exposed. Interestingly, I noticed that some of the strongest students, in terms of grades, tended to be the most worried by the lack of structure. It seemed that they had gotten good grades in the past by learning the expectations and meeting them as closely as they could. I reassured the class often that things would work out and that I was prepared to guarantee that their grades would not suffer, whatever happened, but still the expectation that they would be told what to learn remained very strong.

It also took a lot of time for the learners to put the course together for themselves. I estimate that easily a third of the class time (plus a number of meetings outside class hours) was devoted to organization and logistics rather than actual formal "content." For this particular course, on adult education, this was actually a positive factor, as the learners were having a deeply experiential engagement with the sorts of questions they would have to solve in their practice when they graduated.

Over time the class settled down, worked hard, and completed some extraordinary work. What made the difference in the later weeks of the course was that people started to accept that I wasn't aiming to destroy their GPA just for a principle. When they reached that point, they felt free to follow up on their own interests and explore areas that inspired them. The students' anonymous feedback indicated that they believed they had learned a lot more from the class than from a standard survey of theory and practice. They also said they had gained real insights into the learners' perspective when a more open framework was used, and they would be better prepared for the challenges of this approach.

They made it clear that the potential value of the communication involved in a well-developed and appropriate set of objectives should not be overlooked. If the educator chooses not to supply this framework, the security of learners must be ensured in other ways. In the same way, engagement in the course builds when learners are aware of why they should be engaged, so if you choose not to set out objectives, it is critical to have an alternative presentation of the desired effects of the class. Finally, bear in mind that a more developed relationship between the educator and the learners can allow for a more open approach to the design of the program. Education is a process built on relationships; where these are solid and trusting, the educator can use a wider range of tools.

Solange needs to ensure the highest possible value of the objectives of the course by setting realistic and interesting objectives. She does not have to assess the learners, so there is no need to define learning outcomes, but obviously Cheminvert will be happiest if she leaves participants feeling satisfied with their experience. She decides to set the program up with one highly communicative objective: *After this program, participants will be ready to make three sustainable changes to their building.* She will work with the participants to identify those changes and how people can be prepared to make the best decisions.

THE CONTEXT

As should be clear from the example in the preceding section, context makes a big difference to the way courses need to be designed, and in many cases it can be considered as the most powerful factor. An external body that needs to be satisfied tends to be the major concern of the organization delivering the education, and this is becoming a relatively common situation in education for adults. If your job as an educator is to ensure that apprentice carpenters are able to construct certain types of joints before they start their work experience, then there really are limited options about what sorts of objectives need to be in place for a course. You will still be able to make many other types of choices, but the learners do need to reach a certain point at the end of the class.

This is particularly true when people are being educated toward employment or other involvement in an area where there are legal restrictions around who can work there. As mentioned earlier, Canadian pharmacists have to demonstrate that they meet a wide range of competencies, and there are many benefits to having these competencies fit with the objective of the course. In some teacher education programs every course must demonstrate exactly how students' knowledge is built toward the expected competencies and how the content and assessments fit this process.

There might also be pragmatic reasons for objectives that are not external but driven by the organization itself, such as the need to ensure that everybody completing a particular course is able to perform a certain task. If, for example, you are designing a half-day course on cash handling for new bank tellers, it is reasonable to expect them to be able to handle cash correctly at the end of the course and to be explicit about that objective.

Concerns with standardization can drive objective-based systems. If there is a desire to ensure that every learner is getting a similar preparation, then having the same objectives for each course can go a long way to ensure this. The other side of this approach is that the quality of the educational experience in similar courses taught by different people is easier to assess if all the educators are being asked to work toward the same objectives, so there is the possibility of identifying strengths and weaknesses among the instructors (either individually and privately or as part of professional development and performance review).

Organizations may require clear objectives to be communicated to learners as part of a broader commitment to learner-centeredness. This allows the participants in a class to have the information required to choose a course that interests them and to have some kind of recourse if the class does not do what it claims it will do. This kind of legalistic use of course objectives is not always appealing to educators, but it does offer a potential means to address the power balance between learners and educators to some extent. Informed choices are a key component of increased learner control over their learning.

Generally, the least formal educational contexts are the least likely to require formal objectives. Community-based or leisure courses are more likely to be process-based or topic-centered. However, objective-centered ideas are so powerful that they are coming to be seen as a universal mark of program quality, so even in these areas it is not always simple to leave courses open. Advertising, for example, can drive formalization of objectives, as having a precisely defined outcome can make it easier to communicate to people why they should attend the program.

Online or distance courses are usually at the more formal end of the scale when it comes to objectives, with a very clear framework of expectations and a linear approach to reaching them. Partly this is because there is a need to communicate objectives to learners without face-to-face communication, but in addition the media used in distance education seem to work far more effectively in a highly structured way. While it is possible to have open fora and other mechanisms for highly participative activity online, the overall framework of the course benefits from as much precision as possible.

The resources available to the educator, which vary from context to context, may make a difference to the objectives. If you have limited time and have to create all the materials yourself, tighter objectives may be a way to manage these challenges. If the course is longer and there are more supports, it might be easier to look at things more broadly. Educators often make the mistake of trying to do too much, and objectives can help to narrow the aims to a manageable level.

Solange knows that in her case there is no need for standardization, though it would be useful if she could use a similar type of framework in the future. She is confident that an open objective will provide the direction that she needs while allowing for lots of freedom within the workshop. The benefits that she sees are that it is concrete, communicating the point of the activity very well and fitting with the key expectations of the organization.

CONCLUSION

The way that the objectives of a course should be designed is a somewhat controversial topic, and educators need to decide how they wish to approach it, taking into account the nature of the course and their own position on the issue. In this conclusion, I will return to the questions I introduced in the introduction to the chapter.

Who has the power to decide what the aims of the course should be?

There is the possibility that neither the learners nor the educator have much opportunity to affect the objectives because the power to define them is outside the educational setting. This can be a frustrating experience for all involved and can require a lot of skill and imagination on the part of the educator to translate external requirements into a meaningful plan for the course. Whenever possible, more flexibility should be brought to the process of defining the desired effects of the course, with as much participant involvement as feasible.

How do the available resources affect the aims?

Bear in mind that tighter objectives can help to narrow the range of the course to fit limited time or other resources. A more open educational process can take a lot of time for all involved. The desired aims of the course should take this kind of factor into account and aim to be realistic.

Are there certain types of aims that cannot be brought about by this course?

Sometimes there are good reasons not to have formal objectives or tightly defined aims for the course. If learners are returning to education after many years away, it may be advisable to put the emphasis on the social processes of the group and "learning to learn" rather than specific types of knowledge.

Are detailed objectives for learning necessary?

That depends most strongly on the context in which the course is taking place. If there are external demands for specific course outcomes, it can make a lot of sense to have objectives linked to these outcomes and assessment approaches consistent with this framework. There are also benefits to communication that come from having clear and easily explainable objectives. However, it is perfectly possible to have a course that is defined in terms of the process or the topic and does not include the more formal types of objectives.

How specific do objectives for learning need to be?

If objectives are used, it makes sense to make them as specific as possible. They should also be in plain language that communicates exactly what is expected. Ideally the objective will indicate how it will be shown that it has been met, described in terms of specific things learners will be able to do by the end of the course.

To whom are the objectives intended to communicate?

In highly regulated contexts, the objectives may be intended primarily to show compliance with external requirements, whereas in other cases the intention may be communication with students. This will change how the objectives are developed and how much flexibility is possible in a given course. In any situation, however, the primary function of objectives is communication.

The utility of good objectives that are thoughtfully and well designed is hard to deny in many settings. Equally, the damage that can be done by objectives that are not well constructed and do not fit with the class process can be significant. In this chapter I have tried to provide educators with some ways to think through this design decision, recognizing that, depending on the context in which they work, other factors will be equally or more important. The key message is that objectives are powerful on many levels, especially in communicating intentions and goals, and deserve careful consideration when they can contribute to the aims of the course.

Content and Resources for Learning

RESOURCES FOR LEARNING

How do resources relate to course?

Is the content open or closed?

Do resources need a specific order?

How will resources support learning?

Who should identify resources?

How easy for learners to access?

Henri works for a large insurance company. He has been there for a number of years, and he likes the company a lot. He knows that insurance companies don't have the best reputation, but the one he works for is part of a credit union and genuinely tries to offer good products to its customers at a price that folks can afford. Henri started off as a claims processor, then moved on to office manager and to human resources, and ended up doing a lot of the in-house training offered by the company. It's only part of his job, but he enjoys it a lot. Up till now it's been relatively small-scale, but there's a big challenge coming up.

Due to both the need for cost-cutting and the opportunity to make claims adjusters' lives more interesting, the company has decided that the frontline staff will now have the responsibility to conduct an initial assessment of the truthfulness of callers. To help with this aim, Henri has to train the claims adjusters to use a special system to detect potentially problematic claims. The system is called "Truthhound" and involves asking a special series of questions.

Some of the claims adjusters (he will be working with around fifty in all) have a great deal of experience and have their own tricks for assessing the truthfulness of an insurance claim. Others are very new and either a little naïve or too mistrustful. Some remember Henri when he was a claims adjuster himself, and they view him as a little too big for his boots. Generally, the adjusters see the new approach as a thinly disguised way to get them to do more work for the same pay, and they aren't sure that a system developed elsewhere will even work in their office.

Given the new scope of his responsibility, Henri is a little daunted by the challenge of choosing the content for the course. He is comfortable with the process he wants to use—a mix of presentation and workshop—and with assessment and transfer. He can easily observe to see whether the adjusters use the new system once they have been trained. He is less certain, however, about the content of the course. What should he cover during his two days of training?

The obvious options include looking at fraud generally and discussing what the company currently does, why the new system can help, and how it should be done. But should Henri also talk about the potential cost savings? How can he present the system so that it doesn't sound like he thinks all the clients are crooks? Should they discuss the issue of more work for the same pay, or should he stick to the company line on job enrichment? It might help the staff accept the new system if he could link it to the existing approaches developed informally by the senior adjusters. Should Henri talk to them in advance and try to arrange this?

Henri feels a responsibility to get this right. He believes in the new system and the value of embracing anything that makes an adjuster's job more interesting. He is struggling, though, with thinking through what makes for the best use of content and resources in this complex context.

If you didn't know anything about planning programs, you might think that the central question, the one on which planners spend all their time, would be what to teach and what sort of material would support that knowledge. *Surely*, you may think, *that would be what educators talk about all day!* Yet this is generally not true. The knowledge content and materials tend not to get much attention at all. The central reason is that what the instructor is actually going to teach depends on a range of different factors, so what is taught can vary a great deal from course to course, even if all have the same specific aim or course topic. When I think about content I like to imagine it as a pie (a good cherry pie, in fact). The aim of the course is for everybody to have a chance to eat the pie. However, the ways that it can be sliced by the instructor are infinitely varied, and the range of ways those slices can be eaten, or resliced, or shared by the learners is also huge. The first focus of this chapter is on the way the knowledge content is set and portioned into deliverable slices.

Content and resources are tied together, but in this chapter I am separating the two elements. A good way to know the difference is to think about content as information and resources as objects (even if they are virtual objects such as a video or internet page). So, for example, the content might be "how to make English nouns plural" and the resource in this case would be a worksheet with a list of words. Many times it is quite straightforward to link the two, but in other cases it can be quite tricky.

Resources and materials reflect the intended aims and knowledge content of a course, as well as the teaching process and assessment. Different materials are often used in different ways in different courses, and it can be a challenge to identify the best resources. Currently there are enormous amounts of online resources that can easily be incorporated into face-to-face or online education. Should there be lots of background material or should the material be tightly tied to the intentions of the course? Are worksheets helpful, and if so, how much should they be the focus of the class? One difficult question, in many situations, is how deep the materials should go. (Does Henri really need to start by reviewing the statistics on insurance fraud?)

The questions I will cover in this chapter are:

• How does the content relate to the intended aims of the course?
• To what extent is the content open or closed?

- What are the requirements for the content to be in a specific sequence?
- How will the resources support learning?
- Who should identify and collect resources?
- How, and how easily, can learners access the resources?

A good choice of resources can really bring a topic to life—it can make the difference between a drink of tap water and a glass of fizzy water with a lemon slice! It's well worth putting some thought into this area of course design, but it's important to be clear about what you are hoping for. If you are using the resources simply for the sake of using them, or because you think they are cool, then if they turn out to be ineffective you have far less opportunity to regroup and move on. Making content the more important factor allows for materials to be altered or substituted fairly painlessly. Put briefly, try to avoid teaching *to* resources and aim to teach *from* resources.

INFORMATION AND OBJECTS

One classic definition of content (Houle, 1972, p. 230) is "anything taught or learned in an educational activity, including knowledge, skills or sensitiveness." Nowadays most people would use "attitudes" instead of "sensitiveness," but otherwise this is a very helpful staring point. One striking point about this definition is that it doesn't talk about what is *meant* to be learned; instead, there is an acknowledgment that when we are thinking about the content, we need to acknowledge there will be unintended and incidental learning. People learn a great deal more in and through the interaction occurring in courses than we can predict.

If the educator is working in a context in which the objectives are specified in advance, it can appear relatively straightforward to make decisions about content. But we must be careful about this assumption. It seems like a bit of a silly question, but we need to think about what content is actually for. What does content do? If we consider teaching as being about communication, then content is the "stuff" of that communication. The intention is that this information will relate in some way to a future use. We must maintain a clear line between the aims of a course and the content. The aims of a course are usually an action of some sort, such as expanding knowledge of a topic or being able to do something new. Content is the information people need in order to be able to perform that action. In writing this book, I have tried to work out what sort of information might be interesting and useful and made that into the content. So my aim is that this book will help you to plan your teaching of adults, and the content is information I have selected because I believe it will help you to do so.

Content is actively chosen in the design of a course. It does not magically appear in a nicely organized form; it must be put together in a way that makes some kind of sense, with some things put in and others left out. This process is one of the most political acts in education, and there are many people trying to understand how this process works in schools and other areas of education. When we choose to include information as content in our courses (what schools call curriculum), we are giving it value and importance. Those things that we leave out are being given less importance. While some educators describe their decisions in purely pragmatic terms ("the learners need to know this"), the decisions always have a larger significance.

One example that many people may have read about in the paper or seen on television is the high school language arts curriculum in North American and British schools. When people of my generation went to school in Scotland, we were fed a diet of Shakespeare with a few modern authors thrown in. Currently, the content includes far more Caribbean, South Asian, and African writers. The former way of doing things could easily give the impression that the only writing that was any good was done by dead White men. Including other authors in the content underlines the value of their contributions to literature. This change of content sends a really important message about what counts as valuable knowledge.

Some courses can be very open about the content; others are far more defined. Sometimes the educator has a limited range of choices about content because it is predefined. Driving instruction has a clear and almost universal set of skills and rules you have to know (though there is local variation). Similarly, workplace training very often has specific associated content. Competency-based education for adults generally has, by definition, clear content guidelines. If the content is defined tightly, the educator can focus more on the best teaching approaches to that information than on the content itself.

The opposite situation, with wide-open content choices, is not unusual in teaching adults. Here there is an opportunity to work with the learners in selecting the content. At the start of the course, it may be worth having a conversation with the participants to find out what information they feel they need to know. Even in situations where knowing the content in advance is necessary, a good compromise can be for the educator to present her list of content areas and work with the group to add and to change the emphasis where necessary. The negotiation of content, done well, can be a way to build positive commitment to, and interest in, the course.

Very often a course will include content with different priorities. I was talking recently with a colleague who taught the same course as I did last year, at exactly the same time. Her class had gotten through a huge amount of reading, whereas mine had not done nearly so much. My group had wanted to really focus on the highest-priority information, whereas hers had wanted to explore the topic in depth. Smith and Delahaye (1987) suggest that it is useful, when selecting content, to think about what learners *must* know, what they *should* know, and what they *could* know. In the case of my colleague's class, they were moving well beyond what they had to know and starting to tackle what they could know.

In my own teaching I have come to think of some content as being primary—it is very important that learners know it and it really has to be included—and some as secondary—it will be interesting and useful to some people but is not essential. Over time the secondary content tends to grow as I find new information, while I try to keep the primary content relatively well pruned to ensure that expectations are realistic and manageable. If I am teaching about andragogy, for example, the primary content is Knowles's (1980) ideas and the secondary content is the academic and social context in which he worked. I find this fascinating, but I know that not everybody will—many people will want to understand the ideas but have less interest in their source.

The arrangement of content in a course or program is rarely random. The idea of scaffolding can be helpful in setting out a sequence of information. This is the helpful but straightforward principle, derived from sociocultural learning theory, that learners should start with the simplest ideas and build towards the more complex. So if you are teaching car repair, it is best to talk about changing flat tires before you address rebuilding the transmission, for example. It can sometimes be hard for educators who are subject area experts to order this sequence really well, simply because they are so familiar with the material that they find it hard to judge the relative difficulty of the information. In this case, asking colleagues or the learners themselves to order the content can be very insightful. Sequencing does matter, so it is worth spending time on working out the order in which ideas should be tackled.

RESOURCES AND MATERIALS

Once the content is listed and organized, you now know the information that has to be communicated to support the learning process, at least as far as you can predict. Content comes alive to support learning both through the teaching process, as discussed in the following chapter, and through the materials chosen. Of course, it is possible to work with content with absolutely no materials; the educator could simply stand up and talk, or the group could work together to develop ideas. But in most cases it is far more interesting and effective to have materials to represent ideas and provide a starting point. The work done by materials, however, is always supportive—their role is to present ideas and support learning, not to drive the teaching and learning process.

Materials chosen should always contribute actively to the knowledge generation process. Most of us have suffered through too many long and questionably relevant slide presentation, or read something for a class of some sort only to find that it was never referred to again. The identification of materials, like the prioritization of primary content, requires a degree of discipline and insight. Almost always the key principle has to be "less is more," as a well-selected resource that engages people will be far more helpful than an exhaustive list of everything people could possibly know. It's the difference between reading a story about knights and an encyclopedia entry on castles. Reading the story can easily build the interest to look at the encyclopedia, but for many people simply reading the factual history of castles would lose interest before long.

In some ways, I would rank learner engagement with resources as an even higher priority than absolute relevance or inclusiveness. I always think of a story in *Zen and the Art of Motorcycle Maintenance* (Pirsig, 1974). The main character, at that point a professor, tells a story about asking the class to write about a brick so that they can improve their powers of analysis. The ones who understood the exercise were able to take that topic and explore the entire world. The moral of the story is that you *can* get there from here—beginning with almost any starting point can take you almost anywhere. In teaching adults, we are usually a little more constrained in our choice of starting points, but the same principle holds true. We do not have to search for the perfect material to illustrate a point or to convey information; the way any material is *used* is the most important aspect. If educators accept this idea, it allows a huge amount of flexibility in selection of materials and makes it less important that materials are of a particular type or come from a particular place.

The traditional materials for teaching adults are most often books and manuals. In the twentieth century these were augmented by videos, DVDs, audio recordings, and so on, and more recently the development of the Internet has given each instructor in an appropriately equipped classroom access to an almost infinite amount of material. As universities and technical schools have started posting videos and presentations online, the quality of some of these materials has become very high indeed. Educators should not hesitate to incorporate some of these readily available resources into their work. In a recent class on research, I used an online video on the Tuskegee syphilis trial to make some points about research ethics in a more powerful and moving way that I ever could have with print resources alone.

However, it should be recognized that all of these media are essentially about presenting information and ideas, and that it can be very valuable to work more actively with materials. There is an old saying in education: you don't know something until you have to teach it. The same sort of principle can be applied to materials. By asking the learners to produce content that represents the information they are learning, you cannot only provide an important opportunity for creativity but also ensure that there is deep engagement with the content. That is one of the ideas behind asking small groups to present on topics to the wider class—the process of researching, developing, and delivering a presentation deepens their knowledge and potentially creates a resource that the class can share.

As with many aspects of teaching, there is a great deal of value to diversity in resources. Information can be represented in many different ways, from written form to video to music, and mixing these different modes up a little can bring a lot of energy to a class. I don't mean that the educator should rush frantically from video to workbook to slide presentation and so on, but that different ways to support learning can contribute a great deal to class process and learning. With materials, a little of the right thing is far more valuable than a lot of the wrong thing.

The final message here is that content and materials work together in support of learning. These aspects of the class, alongside teaching approaches, evaluation, and assessment create a whole experience that creates opportunities for people to learn. The educator's role is to ensure that they are all moving in the same direction and that direction fits with the intent of the class.

THE EDUCATOR

Educators who are committed to a student-centered process tend to be more open about content and materials, often building a process of negotiation into their course design. One way to do this is to ask the learners to generate ideas for what they would like to learn. Students often provide content statements such as this one from a trainee hotel clerk: "I'd like to know what to do if a customer dislikes the room they've been allocated and there are no other open rooms." The most efficient way to gather these ideas in a sizeable group is to ask students to work in groups of six to eight to come up with ideas and then build a master list. The art of the educator comes in grouping these statements to build content areas such as "Dealing with unhappy guests." One version of this process is called DACUM (for more information, visit www.dacum.org). However it is done, the key to the process is selecting content areas that complement and do not overlap.

A slightly less open method, but one that still encourages learner participation, is to review a proposed content plan (which can be called a roadmap or something more accessible than "content plan"!) with the learners, and amend it in light of their suggestions. It is not at all unusual to find that there is some content that is essential to some learners but well known to others in the group, and if this is primary content it will be necessary to cover it in some form. This is where the idea of differentiated instruction comes into play, as you can cover necessary information with the group that needs it while others work on something else.

Using any method that allows for a degree of open discussion about content means that the educator will have to sort out materials as he goes along. This is always more of a challenge the first time a course is being taught, but over time it becomes a lot easier. This is also an area where colleagues, if you have any, can be incredibly helpful. In addition, it always impresses me how much the learners know—many times they can identify items they have found appropriate and clear and that can be shared with the class.

There are good reasons why educators may prefer a more closed approach to content. It may be that certain content will mesh well with the teaching approach and assessment processes chosen for the course. The educator may have extensive experience with a particular area and know that certain things really are primary content, even if it does not necessarily appear that way at the start, and that other things that the learners see as essential actually have a lower priority. In this kind of situation, an open process may lead the class astray, and it can be helpful for the educator to explain the content choices she has made. As an example, I always teach "the history of modern thought" in half an hour during research classes. Most learners, if asked in advance, would not identify this as an essential topic as they prepare to undertake a small research project, but I know from experience that the information will be brought up again and again throughout the course. In this case, I choose a more closed approach based on repeated experience.

It is easy to assume that the more technical the aims of the course are, the more closed the content must be. While this is generally true, it is not a universal truth. Even though the course may be based in a specialized area, the aim may be to support problem-solving skills, for example. In this case, the problem of selecting and prioritizing content in an open process may be a really useful part of learning in itself.

The materials that support the content can be found from a wide range of sources, but it is important to acknowledge that convenience is one consideration for educators. Most of us teach a lot and have little time to prepare, so a textbook can be very attractive. Used well, it can help a lot, but it's important to avoid simply restating what is in it. I try to view textbooks as a bound set of handouts, breaking down the text and making it work in the class rather than just assigning readings. On a related topic, worksheets tend to be seen as potentially condescending to adults, but when they are done well and designed at an appropriate level, they can be really useful. Just try not to distribute distant copies of materials written by typewriter in the closing days of the last century—professionalism in materials matters a lot.

As you move through your career as an educator, you will build up a library of content and associated resources that you have found useful and that you return to many times. As this collection grows, so will your flexibility and ability to deal with diverse learners.

Henri is not in an enviable position as an educator, as he has to find a way to gain credibility with the team he used to be part of. The content and resources are already set by Truthhound, but he needs to make good decisions about how to use the resources and which parts of the new system to emphasize. After some thought, he decides that he needs the credibility of the outside company and also needs to recognize what he and his colleagues know about the job. He decides to use a problem-based approach, asking for scenarios from the group and then providing information on the Truthhound solution to the problems identified.

THE LEARNERS

No set of content or resources has any value if it is not effective for the learners. This has to be the final deciding factor in judging how well these elements of your design are working. Even on a session-by-session basis this can change, due to factors outside of your control. Suppose, for example, there is a terrible snowstorm when you are due to meet with the learners, and a class has to be cancelled. You will have to adjust the content to deal with less time to work with learners. The nightmare of many educators is the opposite—what if people move through the content really quickly and there isn't enough left to fill up the available time?

A very useful insight to apply here, from the design literature, is that good design is adaptive (Simon, 1981). That is, you do not pretend to know everything and to be able to predict exactly what will happen. Instead, you design for maximum flexibility and adaptability. I am sure that we have all had the experience of a trainer in the workplace who runs through a pre-set script even when it is obvious, fifteen minutes into a three-hour session, that the content is not appropriate (usually because there's too much and it starts a little too basic). When in this situation as a learner, it strikes me that maybe the trainer has nothing else to say and is locked into a rigid presentation, come what may. We don't want to do that to the learners we work with, so the ability to adapt is crucial.

The learning career of the participants matters a great deal. Not only will their starting points be quite different, but their expectations regarding content also may vary. Those with more formal education may expect more of a textbook approach to a formal set of knowledge, whereas those with other backgrounds may prefer a more open or hands-on approach. These expectations and preferences are going to make a significant difference to the class, so it is good practice to take them into account. As with many aspects of course design, the best approach may be to start with an educated guess and then ask the learners themselves about what is useful content.

A primary consideration in ensuring that the materials are useful in supporting learning is very simple—accessibility. The first aspect of accessibility is that participants have to be able to get resources. More formal approaches such as textbooks, manuals, and so on often have a great advantage here. Once the learners physically acquire the resource, they have it and can always refer to it. One challenge of using a variety of online resources such as videos, documents posted online, web pages, and forums is that you must ensure that all the learners have easy access to the material, ideally at home as well as in class. This means they must own a computer and have an internet connection, and even today this cannot be assumed. For people who do not have easy access to these resources, the course can become frustrating and lose a lot of value.

The second aspect of accessibility can be harder to judge. Even when learners can get the materials, are they able to use them? We've probably all heard the tales of literacy materials aimed at beginning readers with instructions that are available only in written form, and this epitomizes a genuine challenge. The type of materials that people can understand at the start of the course will likely be very different from what they can understand at the end, and just like content, the sequencing can be important.

I've already mentioned the possibility that learners can find and suggest materials that they like, but another interesting option is for them to create materials for themselves and each other. One group of class members who knows a lot about a topic could produce a briefing sheet for others. This has a number of advantages. It respects and solidifies the knowledge that people bring to the class, ensures that the materials are up to date and focused, and supports a participatory process.

As should be fairly obvious from the comments here, I am a big fan of collaborative content and resource selection whenever possible. There are many excellent ways to reach a specific outcome, and it seems to simply make sense to take into account learners' knowledge—not least, of their own preferences and strengths—when making decisions about which route might be best.

Henri is recognizing the knowledge of participants by letting them set the problems for the workshop and then responding to them. Because of the political situation, he wants to retain a little control, but he is making sure to act respectfully toward his colleagues to avoid accusations of behaving arrogantly. The resources come from the Truthhound Corporation, and Henri will make sure that they are ready for the workshop. This is a big cultural change, and it is important that people fully understand the new approach. Overall, his content and resources will be designed to incorporate the techniques developed by more senior colleagues, which Henri sees as potentially compatible with the Truthhound system.

THE CONTEXT

The context in which you are working may have a considerable influence on the content the course has to cover and the materials used in support of that content. While there certainly will always be areas of any program that are open and can be shaped by the participants, the extent to which this is a possibility will vary considerably. In the majority of education for adults there will be fairly strong guidelines for content. The discussion of how to design content and resources does not contradict this but aims to provide guidance on how to use the available freedom as well as possible.

Statements about content make an assumption about the way education works. They assume that you can transplant an activity from a noneducational context into an educational context without fundamentally changing the meaning of that activity. If there is a professional development presentation at a conference, for example, the assumption is that listening to somebody describe how to perform a task can be meaningfully linked to actually doing it in the workplace. This assumption can remain very strong across many different teaching approaches and contexts (as will be discussed in Chapter Nine, on transfer of learning). Whether this assumption really holds—and when and why—is a very important question in education.

The point is, the meaning comes from the connections that the educator and the learners build together. Even when the content and the materials are specified very tightly, the participants in learning have to make them engaging, appropriate, and helpful. Your responsibility as an educator to work thoughtfully and constructively with content does not end just because these aspects of the course are prespecified; there is still an expectation that you will work creatively and effectively with what you are given.

Content is commonly specified to ensure a degree of consistency across programs and courses as well as ensuring that certain content is covered. When training pilots, it's good to know that they can all land in the rain! It's very appealing to assume that having the same guidelines for content will ensure a consistent experience for all learners, but it is not always possible to assume that identical learning will come out of it. People learn different things from identical content, as it meshes with their experience, interests, and motivation in different ways. So identical specifications for content make a good starting point where consistent learning is required, but they do not guarantee it.

The subject matter is an influence not only on the actual content and materials but also on the form that they can take. It does not make a lot of sense to read a book about knitting and consider that an effective learning process. Apart from anything else, it does not seem likely that the kind of folks who would be attracted to a course on knitting would be content to study it in an abstract form. Certain courses, with their associated content, will require particular resources or special provision for learning—one reason why it costs so much to become a doctor is the cost of labs and all the other technical resources that are necessary. If it makes sense for the teaching and learning process, it can be appropriate to have no pre-specified content or materials, except in a very general sense, and focus the course entirely on activity.

Context will affect the availability of certain materials and resources. Some of us work in well-equipped spaces with projectors and computers and libraries; others in very simple contexts. This will obviously make a big difference to what can be done. Either end of the scale is not necessarily a problem, but it is certainly helpful to know in advance what sort of context you will be working in and design accordingly.

I would like to close this section with a more subtle point. One challenge in choosing content and materials is locality; that is, it can be important to look at materials and content and where they are from. In Canada, for example, some American materials are incredibly valuable—others are simply not helpful. For example, the positions of indigenous peoples in the two countries are very different, so reading U.S. commentary on issues faced by these populations is not really very relevant and is likely to disappoint and discourage learners. It is essential to look at the cultural appropriateness of the information that you will be working with in the class and the resources to support it.

Henri wants to make sure that the Truthhound ideas are clearly customized to his company, so he reviews them thoroughly to ensure that the company logo is on them and any examples that don't fit are removed. In one or two places he finds that the law Truthhound refers to is different in his setting. After this review, Henri is confident that he has good resources that are likely to work well with the problem scenarios his colleagues will bring forward.

CONCLUSION

Content and resources lie at the heart of the educational process, supporting learning and building meaning in teaching. Although there are often clear expectations for what should be included in—and left out of—courses, rarely is there no room for the educator to make significant decisions about content. This can be a very important area for positive negotiation between all involved in the class, building mutual knowledge and trust.

How does the content relate to the intended goals of the course?

Content should always be a good fit with the aims of the course, so the educator must have the discipline to trim things down. Less is more. The aim of any course is to encourage deep learning of selected valuable ideas, and the selection of content and related materials should reflect this aim. The identification of primary and secondary content can really help here, as you can put items you believe to be valuable but not essential into the secondary area as a further resource for learning and they will not be lost.

To what extent is the content open or closed?

In most cases, courses have some required content and some opportunities for free selection of information and materials. The challenge of content design is to make the best possible use of the available opportunities. Learner time is a limited resource, and one way to respect it is to try to maximize the opportunities for learners to be involved in decisions about content.

What are the requirements for the content to be in a specific sequence?

If the information is cumulative, it can be extremely important to put it in the right order, building from simple to complex or easy to more challenging. Often this is not the case, but it's best to avoid a simple shopping list of "things you should know." If possible, create a narrative for the course—a story arc that provides a framework for the information. This makes it easier to learn and teach by helping to organize ideas.

How will the resources support learning?

Materials should always be at the service of learning, and there should be a point to all the materials being shared with students. Is it to introduce a new idea, expand on previous information, or challenge existing thinking? The purpose should be active, not based on the material for its own sake ("I really like this book; everybody should read it").

Who should identify and collect resources?

Whenever possible, it's good to make this a joint process of both the educator and the learners. People come to class with such great stores of knowledge and resources that it seems a waste not to work with that background.

How—and how easily—can learners access the resources?

Educators should acknowledge that most materials have a cost, whether it's direct, as in a book, or part of a larger expenditure, such as a computer and internet service. For this and other reasons, accessibility needs to be considered.

As a final point, I would like to underline that enjoyment and interest are generally a good guide to content and materials. If people are engaged, they are learning, and that engagement comes from a feeling of connection with the information that they are learning. The way that you select that content and represent it in materials can make the most potentially dreary topic into a fantastic, fun, and effective learning experience.

chapter SIX

Ways of Working Together

METHODS

Who has power to choose methods?

What are learner expectations/preferences?

Is the educator comfortable with methods?

What are the key external factors?

Are some methods inappropriate?

What is the resource's effect on methods?

Lise is a second-language tutor working with young people in a storefront setting in a strip mall. She loves the work, because she loves language, and she finds it great fun to hang out with the teenagers who have come to her city from all over the world. In turn they are fascinated by her parrot, who plays on a perch at the back of the learning center during the day. Lise is always looking for ways to engage the young people more fully in learning, to get them interested and motivated. Many of them should really be in school, but because they moved to her city as refugees when they were thirteen or fourteen, they don't have the language skills to study at the secondary level. Lise knows that they come to the small community learning center because they don't have much to do and the center is warm and friendly. The challenge is how to help them step beyond that into the language learning that will allow them to be successful in the schools and beyond.

Lise's background is school teaching. When she was in teacher's college she was always interested in how community settings worked. She was fascinated by the idea that people could come and learn just because they wanted to, and that this could be in an informal setting close to their home. But when she graduated from her course, she could not find a school teaching job. She's very happy about the way things worked out, but as a new tutor, because she has not yet had a chance to gain teaching experience, she sometimes feels a bit unsure about how to start language lessons with the young people who come into the center. She does know that none of the approaches she learned for use in schools is going to help much.

Lise has no particular preconceptions. She knows it will take something a bit unusual to get the center users interested in learning. They currently communicate well enough for their everyday lives, mainly in the present tense and without too much nuance. But she knows that this is not going to be enough to allow them to work with the public or read even relatively simple texts. She also knows that if they wait a few years until they have a pressing need to learn, it may well be too late to acquire full fluency. She needs to find a process that can lead to learning, however sneaky and indirect that path may be.

Lise has read some books on community-based learning and knows that it has to come from the ground up. She's just not sure what to do to get the groundswell swelling. The young people who attend do seem to have some respect for education, despite their frustration with schools. The participants are deeply attached to their families and want to do well for them and to help them out. She wonders if there is a way that this commitment can be turned into an opportunity to begin thinking about what sort of languages skills the young people might need—and why.

Educators are faced with many choices when it comes to the teaching process. Experience tends to give educators a range of tools they can use to shape their interaction with students as well as a good understanding of what to use when (which can come to seem almost intuitive over time). Experience also tends to give them a back-catalog of horror stories from when things went horribly wrong! This chapter discusses the teaching process with the hope that you can more often expand your toolkit than add to your stock of stories.

It seems to me that our teaching process arises from a mixture of rational planning on the one hand (such as "we'll discuss this, I'll give this input, the next discussion can then . . .") and our own style of relationships on the other. With the best will in the world, our personal approach to other people shines through in our work as educators. Our enjoyment of humor, our sense of detail orientation, our love of discussion, our need to maintain a slightly more formal tone, and so on, all will affect how we manage the relationships between learners and with ourselves. As discussed in Chapter One, this is not necessarily a problem—the trick is to know your preferences and to understand how they can be assets. The approach to the educational process is one of the areas of educators' work where there is the most freedom to act autonomously and make decisions. There tends to be little real monitoring of how educators enact their professional responsibility and commitments. This means that a thoughtful approach is more important than ever.

The questions I will cover in this chapter are:

- Who has the power to determine the process?
- What sort of learner expectations and preferences need to be taken into account?
- How comfortable is the educator with different methods?
- What external factors need to be taken into account?
- Are some methods inappropriate or infeasible?
- How do resources affect the teaching methods?

In the end, the measure of the teaching process is very simple and very pragmatic: does it work? This means more than just that people learned something. It also means that it was a pleasant experience and they felt respected and valued during that experience. But beyond that, as long as the learners judge the process to have been successful, there are few parameters. Lecturing is not inherently better than discussion work, and a slide presentation does not, in and of itself, change a dull and content-free process into an engaging and exciting one. The point here is that you, as an educator, should feel free to create the process that you believe will work for the aims of the program based on your experience and honest reflection about what has worked previously. As we'll discuss in Chapter Seven, this reflection should include what the learners are telling you about the methods and their reactions.

A word of caution before we move into the discussion of different methods and the influences on your choice and design of them. Sometimes when things are not going well in a course, the first reaction of many people (including me) is to assume that there is something wrong with the instructional approach and that I, as the educator, had better change it immediately. This is followed by a short period of panicking as I redesign the entire course in my head on the spot. My caution: often the issue is not the teaching method; it may well be something completely different or even outside the classroom. I've learned that the teaching approach is very important, but it's not everything, and before changing it midstream I should check in with the participants to get a feeling for how it is working and how it might be changed.

THE RANGE OF METHODS

There can appear to be a bewildering number of ways to teach. There are many options when it comes to creating a situation conducive to learning. I could offer a list of these different approaches, but unfortunately it wouldn't be very useful. Educators tend to develop their own approaches very quickly, drawing on and usually blending many different perspectives, and creating these approaches is something that I believe we must do ourselves, through practice. As we think about designing our classes, we need to understand why a particular approach would be more or less useful. What I have tried to do here is provide some insights into what sorts of methods you might apply in particular situations, with the aim of building your competence and confidence in working across methods.

To frame this a little, I've created Table 6.1. This highlights two aspects of each approach to teaching: people and tasks. "People" refers to how the learners will be asked to organize themselves for the purpose of learning. For simplicity, I've imagined that there is a group of learners, but not hundreds. They can be asked to work individually, in small groups, or as one large group. Each of these has advantages and disadvantages. In a large "all in together" approach, some learners can feel as if they never have a chance to speak, as the group can be dominated by a

Table 6.1
Selected Teaching Methods

	PEOPLE		
TASKS	INDIVIDUAL	SMALL GROUPS	WHOLE GROUP
Respond	Journals	Feedback	Lecture
	Blogs	Presentations	Debate
	Presentations		Panel
			Interviews
Create	Research	Problem solving	Twitter comments
	Arts projects	Research	Collective curriculum
		Case studies	
		Presentations	
		Arts-based projects	
Combine	Wikidocs	Comparison	Voting
		Collective response	Q&As
		Role plays	

few loud voices. If people are working individually, however, they may feel isolated and as if they are not really getting the benefit of their fellow learners' knowledge and experience. Small group work is very often the bread-and-butter approach of teaching adults, but it's important to have a reason to put people into small groups and avoid the temptation of using it as a generic time filler.

That point brings me to tasks. While there is a huge variety of things that learners might be asked to do to help them to create and share new knowledge, I believe that they are really being asked to do three main tasks. The first is to respond to some sort of input, as when the educator shows a video and asks for comments and feedback. The second is to create something (a statement or position as much as an object) to represent a situation. An example of this could be when individuals are asked to write a one-page statement on their philosophy of teaching. The task is to take something that they know and create a formal version of it. The third task is a little more complex and tends to happen only in groups, when people are asked to combine their views on a topic or their experience to come up with a collective position. This is typical of the focus groups used in advertising to understand how well commercials are going to work. A group of people are brought together to comment on the commercial, and their ideas are combined to create a rich picture of how people will receive the product in an advertising campaign.

One approach that is missing from the table, and deliberately so, is "discussion." Adult educators sometimes assume that adults will automatically benefit from discussion and, more than this, that discussion is automatically interesting and liberating for the participants because they have a chance to express themselves and share their views. However, as Stephen Brookfield (2005) points out, this is not always the case. Discussion can turn into a competitive activity or one in which it is all too easy for people to feel slighted. Rather than a general discussion, it makes sense to me to have a specific task in mind, so that the task, rather than each person's individual contribution, becomes the focus of the activity.

It is important to acknowledge, as well, that in the twenty-first century the majority of these activities can be conducted online. The dynamics are likely to be a little different, but most of these structures can be adopted without losing their central purpose and focus. In the discussion to follow I sometimes refer to an online technique specifically, but even when I do not, there is almost always a way to conduct the activity using an internet tool. In my recent work on MOOCs, we have been learning about Google hangouts as the online equivalent of breakout groups, and there are many such options available for little or no cost.

The list of activities in Table 6.1, though far from exhaustive, has been compared to a range of sources (Seaman & Fellenz, 1989; Caffarella, 2002; Waldron & Moore, 1991) and does seem to contain many of the most important approaches to teaching process. In the table the allocations of some of the approaches are not necessarily fixed, but I have tried to position them according to where I have seen those methods most often used—for example, case studies are very commonly used with small groups of learners.

Individual

The first cell under the Individual heading contains three techniques used to encourage individual responses to some form of input. Journals have been a traditional way for learners to express their thoughts, either as a literal journal completed over the course or a series of short notes in response to some event. In recent years, journals have come to mean emotional and highly personal reflections, but in teaching they can be more pragmatic and concrete; for example, you deliver a short presentation on measuring tiles for bathrooms and ask people to hand in their responses. Blogs are very similar to journals in the way they work, with each learner asked to do a short posting in response to an input. You can also simply ask each student to evaluate the input, such as the video, and write down what they learned in a sentence or present their response briefly to the class. The same sort of technique can be used very briefly at the end of a class to get impressions of the course—just ask each student to say one word about her experience so far.

For products encouraging individual creativity, the table lists arts-based projects (which includes poetry and visual arts) and research projects. In both types of projects the individual has to come up with a new and different way to express a set of ideas. There are all sorts of ways that this can be done, and it is also well worth asking the individual learners how they want to meet this challenge.

It can be challenging to develop activities that allow individuals to express their ideas collectively without losing their individual voices. One possibility that has emerged in the last few years is wiki documents—online resources allowing many individuals to create a document among them. The final document should collectively represent each person's position to some degree, but the process remains individual because the writers do not necessarily have to interact with each other, only the document. This kind of approach can maintain a diversity of viewpoints while bringing those opinions alongside each other.

Small Groups

Most of the traditional approaches to teaching adults are not individual but bring people together around a common activity or problem. When the educator is using small groups, it is usually because he wants to maximize the involvement of every participant as well as share the small group responses among all the students. Not only does the method chosen have to encourage participation within the smaller group, but it also must incorporate a way to share that work meaningfully across the class. A common miscalculation is to leave too little time for the small groups to share their work, so some end up feeling left out of the process.

Where there is an expectation that small groups will share their ideas with the whole class, two commonly used methods are feedback and presentations. The main difference between the two is the level of structure. If it is feedback, the educator provides input of some sort and then gives the small group some time to come up with a response and share it. For a video on costumer service, there might be a question such as "What was your overall view of this video?" The response can be very open in both form and content.

If a presentation is asked for, there are usually more guidelines given to lead to a more specific result. Here the direction might be "Prepare a five-minute presentation laying out the work habits suggested by the video, when it would be easy to follow the suggestions, any barriers you can think of, and the implications for your work." The increased specificity of the question makes a surprisingly significant difference to the task and to the way the group will work.

There is quite a list of creative approaches that can work in small groups. Research and arts-based projects are the same with small groups as with individuals, except that people are asked to collaborate to develop their work. Problem-solving approaches are often targeted at small groups so that people can use each other's knowledge to support their work. So, for example, the task might be to solve a diagnostic problem in a health class, and not only will working together potentially lead to more accurate diagnoses, but the participants will learn from the discussion why some options have to be ruled out. In case studies, small groups are the most commonly used vehicle because individuals' experience is cumulative, providing a range of perspectives on the issue. When I was studying human resource management, case studies were used a lot—a brief description of a situation was given, along with the response taken by the company, and our group had to say what we thought of this response and how it could be different. I remember how surprised—and impressed—I was by the perspectives and experiences of my fellow learners. They taught me more than the book. Finally, presentations, as discussed earlier, can be a very useful way for small groups to share their understanding.

Small groups are generally a very effective tool for combining ideas and approaches. In my experience learners can really enjoy approaches such as role-plays, where they get to practice applying what they are learning. Even the most self-conscious people tend to loosen up after a few minutes and take advantage of the opportunity to act like the world's worst customer! Comparisons also work well, with the small group members working together to list the variety of ideas about a single topic. The object here is not to reach agreement but just to see how many different views there can be. This can be an excellent exercise to help groups to become familiar with each other and work together, because nobody need fear saying something that is "out of line"—the whole point is to be as diverse as possible! The opposite tack is to look for collective agreement on a question or topic, with the understanding that anybody can veto the outcome. The value of this exercise is not the final outcome, but the process of sharing views. To work really well, this may require an established and comfortable group.

Whole Group

When you are working with a large group, such as a whole class of thirty learners or more, many of the strategies that would work well with smaller numbers would still work but would be extremely time consuming. For example, it doesn't make sense to have that number of people prepare individual presentations. When working with the whole group, the kinds of methods that can best obtain responses are lectures and presentations. The group can then be asked if they have clarification questions or any other comments. One option that teachers of adults sometimes overlook is guest speakers. People like to be invited in to speak, and it can add a lot to a class to have a different voice.

Debates also work well. Many people learned how a debate works at school, but it does not have to be that formally structured. It can be two people taking each side of an issue and presenting the arguments for and against a statement. Then the group votes on which side was most convincing. I find this especially interesting when people speak against their own opinions—it really can help people to see how the other side thinks! In my experience, learners can be a little nervous about the first debate, but then they usually really enjoy them and may even ask for more.

Panel discussions can be a lot of fun—basically it is a live version of a TV talk show, with each person contributing their perspective. Following on from this, it is possible to set up interviews, where volunteers from the group can be interviewed by their peers following an agreed-upon set of questions. Although this can feel a little artificial at first, it quickly becomes interesting and insightful. This is also an option for guest interviewees, with questions prepared before they arrive.

For creative activities, one of the most interesting strategies I've seen recently is to use Twitter and ask people to tweet comments into a shared account that is then projected at the front of the class. The educator or guest might be presenting on a topic and beside them is a live shared conversation on the topic, to which the speaker can respond from time to time. Another option is a collective curriculum, wherein the class as a whole negotiates their own curriculum, including what needs to be emphasized and what can be passed over more quickly.

Activities for combining knowledge include voting on questions (including the use of those classroom "clickers," if they are available) and the question-and-answer format. It is hard to capture the diversity of a big class group (and in this situation, a group of fifteen can be big), and most ways of working with these groups tend to work with majority rule rather than a more subtle approach.

Based on this discussion, it is not surprising that small group work is so popular for teaching adults. It allows for collaboration and teamwork without swamping the individuality of the people involved. However, it does not follow that small group work is always good. Most experienced educators aim for a balance of people and tasks that allows the class members to get to know each other and that avoids long lectures. In my own teaching I try to deliver mini-presentations followed by hands-on tasks and small group work. The best person I have ever seen at achieving this balance was a literacy educator who would tour the small groups working in her classroom and, from brief conversations, identify a topic that would be of interest to everyone. She would then deliver a mini-lesson on that topic and expect people to apply what she had been talking about immediately, both to reinforce the lesson and so they could see the pragmatic relevance.

The most common mistake I see in teaching is the overuse of presentation software. No number of animations will compensate for asking people to sit still for a long period of time. Beginning teachers tend to prepare excessively, and very often this takes the form of extended and highly elaborate slide shows. For some reason, this seems even more prevalent in human resource development and training. My advice would be to keep the presentations to twenty minutes or so, with twenty slides and twenty words per slide. Trust yourself to speak in tandem with the slides. Recently I've gone further; now I make up a slide show and print it out as handouts, use one copy as speaker notes, and don't project the slides at all. I find that not having folks sit in the dark does wonders for their concentration, though that may say something more about my teaching style!

In the next three sections, I will look in more detail at the ways our three factors of educator, learners, and context play out as you work toward balancing tasks and people.

THE EDUCATOR

Given the amount of freedom typically given to educators in the area of teaching methods, the perspectives and preferences of the teacher can make a great deal of difference in the allocation of tasks and people. One of the most important influences on this decision-making process is the aspirations of the educators—that is, what they want to achieve both as educators and with each specific class. Their teaching perspective (Pratt, 2002, as discussed in Chapter Two) makes a huge difference. If you believe in the transmission model, wherein your job is to get a set body of knowledge "across" to the learners, then you are likely to focus more on tasks that require response. An educator working with a more developmental approach will tend to build more creative and combinatory tasks into the process, as will an educator working from a nurturing perspective. Apprenticeship approaches will tend to use role plays and other strategies that mimic real-life demands.

The social reform perspective is very interesting when it comes to teaching methods. There is a real contradiction between the desire to support increased autonomy on the part of the learner and the ambition to share a particular perspective on the world. An example of this comes from my early career as an educator. I firmly believed in the power of education to change people's views of the world and, eventually, to change that world. I was working with a group of unemployed people with all sorts of different backgrounds, including time spent in prison and other difficult experiences. For them, the most valuable social reform would be getting a decent and well-paid job. They were not very interested in learning about the theory of surplus labor as a way to understand why they found it hard to get employed—they just wanted a job. As with so many aspects of teaching adults, we need to strike a balance.

A similar issue can arise concerning the degree of learner-centeredness in the course. To what extent should the instructor "let go" of process—or control it? In the tradition of educating adults, there is a great deal of emphasis on learner control and letting the group have a lot of say in the structure. Although this may be a powerful experience, it does require the educator to have a really clear view of what the class is trying to achieve and how to support that aim with a looser structure than I suspect most of us are accustomed to. Learner-centeredness does not mean stepping back from the teaching process, but rather playing a different role within it. It can take far more preparation and thought on the part of the educator to allow a more open process than to simply deliver a series of mini-lectures and exercises. Facilitating learner-centered learning may mean having multiple options of resources and activity for each class meeting, or having to work with smaller groups on slightly different trajectories.

If learning is understood as a sociocultural process, then it makes sense to use more creative and collective approaches, most often based on learner-centered principles. In this view, learning comes not only from the process but also from the planning and development of that process. Methods calling for responses could even be seen as getting in the way of learning, or at least not making the best use of the social resources in the room.

The experience of the educator also affects approaches to teaching in two ways. First, educators may never have been exposed to certain methods and may simply not think of applying them in the class. Second, the educator may be aware of a method, such as a debate, but not be confident about putting it into practice. In such a situation, I believe that the educator's level of commitment really matters. If you are to take on the responsibility and challenge of teaching adults, it seems to me that you should be a learner yourself and constantly build on your abilities and confidence. One really helpful approach is to share ideas and plans for teaching with another educator, as often they can inspire different ways of doing things and the confidence needed to "give it a go."

Overall, it's generally true that the best approach to teaching methods is to build diversity into the design, with a variety of methods and arrangements of people and tasks. Given the high degree of control that educators have in this aspect of their practice, it can be important to have a range of methods to apply in different situations. I do not believe it is necessary to use a specific approach to recognize a specific philosophical orientation; using a variety of methods offers learners a chance to vary their engagement and process in the class. With experience, many educators develop a style of teaching that permits variety in their approaches without diminishing their underlying consistency of intention and philosophy.

Lise has established a high level of trust with the learners who attend her sessions, which she considers an excellent starting point, but she knows that a clumsy choice of method could undo that very easily. Knowing her own limitations and lack of experience in the area, she decides that the learners can play an important role in helping her decide how to introduce language content. Lise is very clear that for this group the most important criterion for the methods chosen is that they build learner engagement.

THE LEARNERS

When thinking about how to build a portfolio of methods for teaching adults, it is critical to take the learners into account. As discussed earlier, their learning careers will have given them a particular perspective on teaching and learning—especially on which approaches work best for their learning. As an educator, it is important that you acknowledge this history but also consider whether it is better to reinforce or challenge it. For example, a person may have gone through very formal, teacher-centered educational experiences and come to associate that with high-quality education. Depending on your philosophy as an educator, you may want to go along with this idea or provide a range of experiences so that the learners can at least build knowledge of different approaches.

The learners' expectations matter. They may expect a certain approach to teaching, and it is possible that not meeting those expectations could lead to negative reactions to teaching methods even when they are appropriate and effective. For example, in some cultures a highly participatory approach to teaching is never used for serious learning. This means that when a more inclusive approach is used, such as small group research and project work, the learners may initially feel uncomfortable and out of their depth. Often later in the process learners become very comfortable with methods that do not set the instructor up as the "expert," but it is important that educators find a way to bridge the gap and bring people into new and unexpected ways of working. One option is to provide micro-experiences of different methods to learners and build out from there. So a group of learners who are used to authoritarian teachers could be asked to complete small and brief autonomous tasks such as picking a topic for the next class.

This is one of the reasons why learner input into class design (discussed in Chapter Seven) is so important. If you arrange to have some form of feedback from the learners as part of every meeting, it is easy to see which approaches are working and which you should move away from. Learners are often very effective at informing the educator about their views on teaching. Even though there is a power balance at play (especially when you will be assessing their work), adults are often willing to provide honest—and usually insightful—commentary. The only pitfall can be that some learners love an activity (such as debates) whereas others hate it, so the overall class response is not really clear. This underscores once more the need for diversity in teaching methods.

The emotional comfort of learners is, in my view, highly important. A few years ago I took a language course—I was doing a lot of work in Germany and thought I should know the basics of the language. Even after twenty-five years as a teacher of adults, the course quickly reduced me to a paranoid, defensive wreck. Although educators work hard to make sure their teaching processes are supportive, learners can feel so exposed just by being learners that they are paralyzed and struggle to learn anything beyond survival in the class. The methods used for teaching should build emotional comfort and enjoyment and, needless to say, should not create or reflect conflict within the group of learners. Simply observing the learners will quickly reveal what they are enjoying and what they are struggling with.

Generally, learners appreciate active teaching methods, whether that means moving around and rearranging themselves or taking part in a hands-on activity. Though we often hear in the media that people have a shorter attention span now than in the past, it strikes me as more likely that sitting listening to a lecture for an hour was never an interesting or effective way to learn, and rarely enjoyable. Try to get a sense of the pace at which the group wishes to change activities, and try to adhere to it. This is especially important for many learners I work with, who come to classes in the evening after a long day at work. The last thing they want is to sit and listen for a long time. They are already tired, and having to sit still tends to make things worse. Instead, relatively brief and interesting activities, including mini-presentations, seem to work well.

A further point to bear in mind is that some teaching methods require work to be done outside of the official class meeting times. This could be meetings and preparatory work for a group presentation, for example, or written responses to reading. Educators should try not to forget that adult learners have lives and responsibilities outside the immediate learning environment. It is appropriate to vary deadlines and allow learners to design their own process for out-of-class work, if any, rather than assuming that your course is the major priority of their lives.

In my experience, most learners enjoy a wide range of methods. As long as you have the group involved and have built a trusting relationship, they will provide the information that you, as the educator, need in order to plan for tasks and people.

Lise notices that the young people in the center really enjoy talking about the difficulties of moving to the city. She wonders whether, as a first step, they might be interested in creating a guide for teenaged newcomers. At first she is thinking about a short book, perhaps with photos and maps, but it soon becomes clear that the group are interested in the idea only if it's an online resource that can be found through Facebook. She is fascinated by this idea as a way to begin the engagement process, and she decides that, with the permission of the director of the center, that is what she'd like to do.

THE CONTEXT

It bears repeating that the context in which you are working shapes what you can do. The first concern is the degree of consistency expected across classes. When educators enter a new context, they should try to discover whether they are expected to go along with a set of approaches to teaching that is already in place in the organization. Some settings can be very clear that they expect some sort of consistency in their approach; others may leave things wide open. Some companies, for example, have highly defined expectations for professional development, whereas others are open to a range of approaches. Sometimes a high level of consistency is expected because it appears to offer a way to ensure high-quality teaching (and learning). A lot of the standardization in schools is based on this philosophy, and although it does not necessarily follow that "same is better," I think the temptation to adopt this approach is understandable.

If there is an expectation of a consistent approach, it is often described as a "professional" approach to teaching adults. This often means there should be a degree of formality in the approach to teaching, perhaps with an emphasis on methods requiring responses, and that the educators should be prepared to take on the role of subject matter expert in the class. It is easy to imagine a corporation, for example, requiring a consistent set of methods for teaching new middle managers about accounting procedures. This is not a problem at all—until it starts to turn up in places where it is not helpful. Having a standardized approach to teaching French to immigrants when the class is composed of people with different first languages, different knowledge of French, and different levels of schooling is clearly not going to be too helpful. Consistency needs to be tempered with an appreciation for the realities and complexities of human learning.

The idea that teaching approaches can, in and of themselves, guarantee the quality of learning is very common but does not represent a good understanding of education. If I am evaluating a teaching situation, I view responsiveness to learner needs—far more than consistency—as a marker of quality. However, it is also fair to say that if learners are taking three courses and those courses are wildly divergent in their teaching approaches, this may strike the participants as disorganized and lacking coherence. I have become more committed in recent years to the importance of educators working together so there is a flow and a degree of relatedness between classes likely to be taken by the same people (such as a set of entry-level health care training courses). I do not believe it is viable for educators who are working with the same students to adopt completely different approaches and appear credible. If you are teaching a stand-alone course, then you do not have to worry about overlaps and gaps and have the opportunity to be highly creative and eclectic in your approach.

A lot of the discussion in this chapter has assumed there are no concrete reasons not to pursue a particular teaching method, but in real life, of course, resources are a key consideration. The hardest to deal with is time. If you are teaching a six-hour course, you do not have a lot of time to build cooperating small groups and plan a collaborative curriculum. As discussed earlier, if the learners can only commit to the actual time in the classroom, then this is a real, hard limit to what can be achieved. It is the mark of an accomplished educator to use time well, which usually means not excessive planning and ending up having to rush through things. Better an early lunch or a short session than going over time and having to cover five new items in the last five minutes as people pack up. This leaves no time for feedback and often feels disrespectful to the learners.

Two other types of resources are worth bearing in mind. One is the space you are working in. A room with seating like a cinema will be hard and uncomfortable for group work, and a room with pillars and separate tables with seats around them (cafeteria seating) is not great for front-focused presentations. So it's well worth looking at the room and thinking about what feels easy and natural within that space. The second type of resource is the general teaching support, ranging from flip charts and markers through LCD projectors and online resources. It can be enormously frustrating to be working in a room with fifteen square meters of whiteboard—and no working marker pen! Make sure that you have what you need to support the methods you want to use.

While context can be, and often is, relevant to some degree in the educator's selection of method, in most cases you have a lot for freedom to teach the way you think is important and helpful. Most contextual factors need to be acknowledged and built on rather than seen as absolute barriers to your practice.

Lise's director likes the idea of the website and Facebook resource, but Lise finds out that the center cannot allow Internet access through its own computers in case the young people accidentally access question-able sites. She notices that there is an open WiFi signal in the building and decides that it is easier to get forgiveness than permission. Working with her own laptop, Lise and the group begin to create the OurTown website to welcome newcomers, editing and correcting each other's writing and starting to have conversations about why language matters.

CONCLUSION

Teaching approaches are often seen as the heart of education for adults. In this chapter I have approached them as just one set of design decisions existing alongside the others. I have tried to avoid giving more than a very short and indicative list of the sorts of methods available to educators, as there are many such lists available, and I think it is far more important to point to some potential ways to choose the methods. This brings us back to the questions in the introduction to the chapter.

Who has the power to determine the methods?

In most cases, the educator has a huge amount of discretion to select the teaching approaches that he believes would work best in that particular context. In more learner-centered approaches, this power can be shared with the class participants. Only rarely, however, are the key instructional decisions not made in the classroom.

What sort of learner expectations and preferences need to be taken into account?

The key to answering this question is having an approach that recognizes the need for emotional security and enjoyment as well as the diversity of meanings this need may have for the groups of learners. If people have specific expectations about the class process, it can be important to know these even if your intention as an educator is somewhat different. Building a relationship with learners is a central concern as you develop the class process.

How comfortable is the educator with different methods?

It is vital that the educator feels that she can facilitate the type of learning she is aiming for, effectively and comfortably. Diversity of teaching strategies is so important that it truly is central to who you are as an educator. Though educators may not want to tackle methods they are unsure of, willingness to do so is a great indicator of the potential to learn and to strengthen your practices as an educator.

What external factors need to be taken into account?

There is not a long list of possible factors here, but you should recognize learners' expectations of consistency or a particular way of presenting material. Even if the expectations do not fit your style and philosophy, being aware of them is a necessary step in working with them.

Are some approaches inappropriate or infeasible?

Sometimes the desired approach is just not going to work. Lecturing a group of people who have not completed schooling about the importance of correct grammar is not appropriate or helpful. Be aware that sometimes the fit is bad, and be ready to move on.

How do resources affect the teaching methods?

Resources are a hard limit on teaching methods. Unless you want to pay for resources yourself or are in a powerful enough position to get whatever you ask for, you can expect that lack of some resources will be a factor in your planning. Happily, teaching processes have enough flexibility that there is usually a way around the limitations.

In this chapter I have approached teaching methods with the view that they depend on the relationships among the educator, the learners, and the context. Building a good relationship with learners, in which they can provide feedback on what is and isn't working, is one of the most significant steps in creating a set of experiences that will support learning and move learners toward the aims of the course. The educator's role is to facilitate this, much as a conductor works with an orchestra, sometimes getting close and detailed, other times giving overall guidance for how she wants the piece to sound and trusting the instrumentalists to know how to achieve the effect. In the end the educator uses methods as a frame, then participates in the dynamic processes of interaction as the groups work together to create the learning process.

Department of
Adult & Community Education

chapter SEVEN

What Do the Learners Say?

LEARNER INPUT

What insights do learners have?

What needs to be known?

How frequently is input needed?

Is comparability needed?

Is the focus experience or learning?

What are resources for evaluation?

Who leads the evaluation?

Instructors want to know what their students think of the class. They are interested in how much the participants are enjoying it and whether they think they are getting anything useful out of it. Unfortunately, the students' judgment of the class is sometimes affected by their judgment of the instructor. Susanna is all too aware of this. As an instructor in a trades program, she is unusual because she is a woman. Not many girls grow up with the passionate interest in machinery, especially cars, that Susanna has had as long as she can remember. She knows that the young men coming through the program sometimes don't give her the credit she deserves for decades of work in the auto parts trade and the vast knowledge she has built up. (If you are going to put a four-barrel Holley on your classic SS, she can tell you how much you have to upgrade your fuel pump to keep it happy.)

One place where she differs from the other instructors is in the kind of talk she will—and won't—tolerate in the class. The other instructors put up with a lot of salty language and humor that seems to Susanna to be on the wrong side of the line. This puts her in the position of appearing prudish to some of the students, and she believes the student evaluations are affected by this perception. Though she understands the students' point of view, Susanna still thinks it unfair that she is being punished by the students for not encouraging behavior that is sometimes sexist and racist. She believes that the other instructors play up to the students in a patronizing way.

The bigger problem she faces is the difficulty of getting good information out of the students regarding her teaching style. She would love to know, for example, whether they find the videos she uses in class interesting and useful and whether she should include more internet resources. The challenges of her relationship with the students are getting in the way of good information about what they are learning and how much they are enjoying it. She is just not sure how to go about finding out what they think. The end-of-course evaluations come too late and do not give the detail she believes she needs to improve her teaching.

Susanna is looking at the options, trying to find a strategy to get the perceptions of students in a reliable and pedagogically useful way. She believes that she generally does a good job with the classes, but she needs to get past the students' opinion of her as a person to understand their view of her as a teacher. She looks forward to finding a way to discover how the students really feel about her classes, and what she could be doing better.

When we talk about evaluation, we are talking about a whole range of different processes with diverse motivations. However, it comes down to the basic question of finding out how well our instruction is supporting student learning. Who is asking the question changes the types of evidence that should be used, how it will be collected, and the implications of the question. In keeping with my commitment to sociocultural learning, this chapter emphasizes the value of learner insights into the teaching and learning process as critical information in designing that process.

The next chapter looks at how the educator can collect evidence on student learning through assessment, and Chapter Nine looks at how we can build bridges between our teaching and the contexts in which participants might use what they learn. These three topics are clearly closely related, but in the current chapter the focus is very much on the ways you can understand the value of your teaching for learners. Evaluation, in this discussion, means gathering the perspectives and insights of participants regarding the teaching and learning process in order to improve that process.

There is a second use of the term "evaluation," not discussed here but useful to know about. It is often referred to as "program evaluation," and it is sometimes conducted by people outside the educational organization. As the need to demonstrate effectiveness in publicly funded programs has grown, a new profession specializing in evaluation has sprung up. In this situation, evaluative information goes beyond the data you gather to inform your teaching directly. It can also be used by funders and other sponsors to assess the effectiveness of the course, and it is important to pay attention to this function. It may not be possible to keep the program running if you cannot demonstrate that it is delivering the outcomes that have been agreed to. In addition, sometimes organizations see evaluation information as a way to understand the quality of teaching and learning in the course, and even how well the educator is doing her job. There is a lot of available information on what we can consider "external" evaluation, and it goes well beyond the scope of this book. Here we stay focused on directly using learners' insights to inform teaching.

Over the last few years there has been mixed progress in the techniques educators can use to capture the views of learners. Very formal settings have moved toward tools such as anonymous online questionnaires. In less formal settings there is still a tendency to use very simple evaluations asking how satisfied learners were with the course. The options open to the educator for gathering participant input will vary depending on where they are working, but there is almost always room for a great deal of individuality and creativity in the tools available to assess how well the class is working for learners. I encourage responsible educators to take advantage of this freedom and do the best possible job of drawing together this critical information.

The questions I will address in this chapter are:

- What insights do learners have into teaching and learning in this setting?
- What needs to be known about the course?
- How frequently is input into the course design needed?
- Is comparability between different courses needed?
- Is the focus on learner experience or demonstrated learning?
- What sort of resources are available for evaluation?
- Who is going to be in charge of leading and developing the evaluation process?

Whatever approach to evaluation is taken, the insights of learners are always a key component of teaching adults. A well-thought-out method for incorporating participants' perspectives can signal your seriousness about building the course around the experience of learners in a very powerful way and will also provide information that you need to know as an educator. It is far easier to respond to feedback early in the course than to wait until the end, by which time the learners may be fed up and the educator wondering what went wrong. The value of a clear line of communication among all the stakeholders in a course cannot be overestimated, and a good evaluation strategy can be the centerpiece of that communication.

DESIGNING EVALUATION

The topic of this chapter is how educators can learn about learners' reaction to the learning setting and their general satisfaction with it. I use the term "input" when I'm talking about learners' contributions because I believe that it adds weight to the information that we get from learners, and it implies that educators will take it into account and do something about it. Put simply, input is the range of information that we get from learners regarding the program, including suggestions, their judgments of the approach you are taking, and the other experiences they may want to share. Adult learners often have a lot of input to give, and the educator in this situation should consider that input an important asset.

A teaching and learning situation, whether it's a formal classroom or community group, is a complex phenomenon. Educators need to be able to respond to relatively subtle currents within that situation, and learner views are an essential component. There is a double purpose to evaluation. First, the educator can get a sense of the affective positions of the learners—are they liking the class? This provides good information on engagement and motivation. Second, educators can get feedback on concrete aspects of the learning process. For these reasons, educators can benefit a great deal from understanding and applying effective evaluative methods.

I'd like to offer one word of caution. The job of evaluation would be a lot easier if participants' impressions of the course were a reliable indicator of high-quality learning, but unfortunately this isn't the case. Sometimes people love classes, have great fun, and then forget everything the minute they walk out. On other occasions, learners find classes uncomfortable and challenging but come to appreciate what they learned over a longer period. A great example here is learning to drive. Nobody would seriously say that they enjoyed learning to parallel park—it is stressful, the driving instructor is right there watching every move, and other motorists are waiting for you to get on with it so that they can get to where they want to go. Yet every day that I have driven since I passed the test I've been glad that I learned this skill. Immediate enjoyment and long-term impact often seem to be linked quite loosely, at best.

There is a considerable amount of research on this question, especially within universities. Because they are some of the most structured educational environments, with students essentially a captive audience, it should be relatively straightforward to look at the relationship between people's reactions to classes and the long-term impact. The students' formal evaluations of the course are used in a lot of these studies to represent their immediate reactions, and their grade is used to represent the long-term learning from the course. The question is, how related are these two factors? Can we assume that the immediate reactions of learners give us a good guide to whether and what they have learned? Well, there seems to be *some* relationship, and generally good evaluations do seem to suggest that folks have learned something. However, this relationship is complicated by a long list of factors such as different views of what good teaching looks like; the difficulty of the course; the grades people think they will get; the gender, ethnicity, and background of the instructor and the students; and so on (Clayson, 2009; Spooren, Brockx, & Mortelmans, 2013). Given the number of complicating factors, educators cannot really claim that good evaluations of the class by students alone serve as proof that learners have learned a great deal. We must decide what counts as a good course—is it indicated by happy students or by strong performance on any assessments that are included? Educators should make sure they and the students are clear on this point throughout the design and delivery process.

When setting out to collect information from students regarding the course, a few points must be taken into account. Sometimes educators wait until the end of the course before asking for any evaluation. Then on the last day they hand out a sheet of paper with a number of checkboxes and things to circle. I think this is a mistake. As an educator, I really do believe that I learn from every group of adults with whom I work, and I'm not going to learn very much if I wait until the very end of the course to ask people what they think—and then limit their answers. Evaluation should be built into the class from the beginning and flow through the entire process. It is critical that educators acknowledge the input of learners and tell them how that input will be addressed. So, for example, learners often give very strong input on logistical issues such as when breaks should be, and quite frequently half of the feedback is that the break is too long and the other half is that it is too short. I often handle this by sharing the input with the class at the next session, and I tell them quite seriously that this indicates to me that the length of the break is probably about right. So even if nothing changes (for a good reason), people do get the message that I read their input and think about it.

To get good information, it is important to ask not only about the history of the course so far (as in "What were the most helpful points from my presentation on fuel injection?") but also about what could or should be changed. Generally, evaluations should be more future-oriented until the final one looks back on the course as a whole. A very simple but effective approach that I learned from my colleague Kathy Maclachlan is to distribute a sheet to learners with three headings: "Start," "Stop," and "Continue" (traffic light colors can also be used). In choosing which heading to place a comment under, participants naturally tend to provide input on how the course could fit their learning better. They draw on their experience to that point without having to list it explicitly. This technique and similar ones can be very powerful; and, as with so many aspects of teaching, the simpler the better!

Anonymity is a key issue in evaluation. People can be very unwilling to share their thoughts about a course in a conversation with the educator or with other learners present. In either case, people can feel that they are very exposed. I have observed this a lot, and I have come to the conclusion that people's unwillingness to speak directly to the educator about their experience in a formal course (other than to say politely "It's good" and then not elaborate) is not because of the obvious fear that it might affect their grade. Rather, I think that the educator and the learners are involved in a situation in which both sides want to be successful, and we have learned to talk only positively in such situations. This also applies in situations where there are no grades to take into account. Conducting evaluation anonymously can remove this barrier and make it much easier for people to give their thoughts openly. When there is a high level of trust between the educator and the participants, it's possible to discuss the progress of the course openly without the concern that learners will worry about consequences. But even here, you cannot be as confident that people are responding straightforwardly as you would be with an anonymous approach.

If the educator opts for a more open approach, such as asking the whole class for feedback toward the end of each meeting, he could use one of two strategies I have found to be helpful. The first is to ask specific questions about the course. Instead of asking "How is it going?" or "Am I teaching this well?," ask (for example) "Did that exercise help you to understand valve timing?" Depersonalizing the process and asking a detailed question supports the idea that learners and educators are working together to clarify what is effective. It's important to avoid the perception that critical comments on class process are a personal attack on the educator. The second strategy is to have fun with it. For example, you may ask people to stand in a line across the room, with one wall as "strongly agree" and the other as "strongly disagree." Then ask them to arrange themselves depending on their response to a statement like "The practice we did this week will help me to remember how to weld."

By thinking up ways for learners to express evaluative judgments in a light-hearted way, the educator can take a lot of the anxiety out of feedback, which leads to more useful and honest information. There are a range of useful ideas for evaluation in books such as *Planning Programs for Adult Learners* (Caffarella, 2002), but I think it is best for educators to build their own portfolio of methods over time. Many educators who work with adults are able to draw on a range of different approaches in different contexts, which is an enormous asset. For those new to teaching, having five or six ways to capture student feedback that they really like and find effective can be enough to get started.

In designing ways to collect evaluation information, it helps to weave them into the course as fully as possible. Evaluation is not something that the educator can come to when everything else is in place (Caffarella, 2002); instead, it should be viewed as central to the learning environment. I can think of very few examples of courses where some form of evaluation is not an intrinsic part of the learning environment—or could usefully be.

THE EDUCATOR

For educators, evaluation is not just a technical process, however much we build techniques around it. At the heart of evaluation lies judgment—and the fear that people will be making a statement about the effectiveness of our teaching. It is easy to take this as a judgment of the educator as a person rather than feedback on the process, particularly because teaching is such a personal act (as I've suggested throughout this book). It would be naive to suggest that from time to time learners do not allow their view of the educator to influence their feedback, but this can be minimized through careful design of evaluation instruments. Educators who want to use evaluation information effectively need to find a way to depersonalize it and accept it as something that they can learn from—in other words, as a unique and incredibly valuable opportunity for professional development.

Entering into evaluation with a good level of openness helps avoid one of the most human of traits: focusing on the negative. I am as vulnerable to this as anyone. When I read my teaching evaluations, whether at the end of a course or during the process, I'll always remember the less positive comments. If nine people say they like my sense of humor and one person says I'm not taking the course seriously, that person will be the one I believe. Partly, this is because I know that people tend to tell educators relatively nice things and therefore I take the positive comments less seriously, but partly I think it reflects an assumption that we really *can* please all the people all the time—and should be doing so! As a way of dealing with this tendency, I look for patterns across comments and, where possible, across different courses I have taught. When four or five people in three courses are telling me that something is not working, I will take that pretty seriously. So alongside openness, educators need to avoid bringing oversensitivity to the evaluative process.

Some of these challenges can be reduced by being as specific as possible in the questions asked in student evaluations of learning. You are trying to generate information about concrete aspects of the course from the students' perspective. You can then use that information to make changes in your practices. You do want to understand how satisfied people are with the course in general, but if you don't have information on the more concrete aspects, you can't understand why people feel that way, and you won't be able to make things better. One important aspect of evaluation and being able to ask about concrete aspects of a course is knowing different ways to gather information from participants. Each way of inviting input will gather some insights from some perspectives, but to develop a rounded overview you must ask the questions a number of times, being as specific as possible.

An example of this approach is an evaluation sheet that focuses entirely on the activities in a specific class session. It would run through each activity one at a time, asking questions like "What did you learn from this activity?" and "How could that learning be reinforced?" The last section of this sheet would ask for a judgment about the session as a whole to provide insight into satisfaction with the class. The evaluation is concrete, focused, and respectful of the perspectives of learners, as well as being repeatable without redundancy.

Educators should pay attention to the satisfaction of the learners with the course not only because they want people to be happy (which I hope we all do) but also because learners who are less content are going to be less motivated to learn. They will not participate as effectively in the course, and they likely will be far less willing to share their own experience and insights. The affective dimensions of engagement in learning are profoundly influential on learning outcomes (for a useful overview of this topic, see Kraiger, Ford & Salas, 1993), and can be seen as underpinning the entire educational process. Relationships in a teaching and learning setting need to be respected and developed in order to support an authentic process of exchange and development. When it works, this creates a virtuous circle whereby participants become happier with the class, are more motivated to engage, learn more, and become more satisfied. Educators who want to support this upward spiral are often aware that their own reading of the class is not enough and that they need to request and respect the views of the participants. A good evaluative method does this.

Susanna decides that she needs to design her evaluations to target the specific thing she needs to know about the design of the class. She develops a video feedback sheet that she asks learners to complete after every third or fourth time she uses audiovisual material. She finds that simple scales get a good response, but open questions with room to write a short response tend to get one-word answers. So although she understands which resources the participants find useful, she does not really know why.

THE LEARNERS

Asking for feedback on our practice as educators is not an easy thing to do, and it's not easy to give that feedback, either. There are a number of aspects to which the educator can pay attention when designing evaluation that can make the process easier and more valuable for both sides.

One aspect that makes a significant difference is the credibility of the evaluation method chosen. Credibility comes from two qualities of the method. The first is that the information gathered is the right information. Learners are unlikely to be impressed if the evaluation for a very formal course asks about nothing but feelings. Equally, an informal, community-based program that tries to collect standardized information through multiple-choice questionnaires would likely strike participants the wrong way. Credibility requires that evaluations demonstrably attempt to gather data that is a good fit with the learners and their reasons for being there.

The second dimension of credibility is that the evaluative data has to be put to use. This is true both for ongoing evaluation, such as session-by-session input, and for final evaluation of a whole course. The educator needs to be able to explain what the information is for and what sorts of changes may come out of it. Nobody wants to invest the time and effort to complete an evaluation process if it won't make any difference.

If the evaluation lacks credibility, people will not put the thought into it that the educator hopes for. Instead, they will try to rush through it as quickly as possible. People who design standardized tests have a clever trick to catch this—they reverse a question or statement every so often. So, for example, ten statements have "strongly agree" as a positive response and the eleventh question might ask the learner to respond to the statement "This class is incredibly boring." Somebody who simply chooses "strongly agrees" for everything on the sheet will create a logical inconsistency that is easy to catch, and their responses can be discounted. Unfortunately, there is no such easy catch for other types of evaluation.

Clarity goes along with credibility. Learners often have little patience for an evaluation question that is vague. Although educators sometimes think that they are leaving lots of room for an expanded and open response, the learner may experience this as annoyingly unclear. Try to avoid questions such as "How has your development as a speaker and writer of French evolved over the course of our program?" When I am a learner, I don't want to have to decode the question. Ask me "How much do you think your oral expression has improved through in-class exercises?" and I'll have a good stab at answering because it's clear what the educator is looking for and there is an implied use for the information.

As discussed earlier, I do think that on balance anonymity is almost always a positive factor in learner evaluations of educators, not least because of perceived power imbalances. However, there is a useful subtlety here. As with research, sometimes the goal does not have to be complete anonymity, and "plausible deniability" is enough. This means that the evaluation tools can be designed to be unidentifiable, such as when a handwritten sheet is passed around for each learner to complete by hand. It cannot really be characterized as completely anonymous—the educator could work out whose it was by looking at the writing, the pen used, and so on—but it is also easy for the learner to deny that it is her submission. In some cases that extra layer of distance from the evaluation information is enough to provide a level of comfort for the learners.

Frequency of evaluation can be quite an important consideration. A balance can be struck here. The educator needs to get feedback often enough that he can respond to it during the course of a class, but without trivializing the whole process. Often I start off with frequent evaluations at the start of the course—maybe even at every meeting. But these evaluations are very simple and easy to complete and as varied as possible. Once the course is under way, I'll evaluate every second week or so. By obviously responding to the information gathered early in the course, the educator can set a good direction and tone early on.

I will close this section by looking at one of the myths of evaluation. When people are conducting evaluation in formal settings, one recurring question is whether "tough" instructors tend to get worse evaluations. That would imply that even though the learners might learn better from a more rigorous teacher, the teaching evaluations would not be as strong as for a teacher with lower standards. When this question was researched, it turned out that teaching evaluations are linked to learners' *perceptions* of learning but not necessarily to their *measured* learning (Clayson, 2009). In other words, instructors get good scores when participants *think* they are learning. In addition, learners' perceptions of learning are highly varied and subjective (Spooren, Brockx, & Mortelmans, 2013). The moral of this story is that even though evaluation of teaching by participants can provide essential insights, it is as partial and personal as any other information about your teaching, and it should be considered alongside other factors. It should be accepted as serious input and responded to responsibly, but you probably cannot become a better teacher just by improving your evaluation scores.

In reflecting on the reasons for the lack of input from the students, Susanna realizes the students may be thinking she lacks credibility. Because she is seen as a bit strict, they may not trust her or believe that she will change anything on the basis of learner input. She realizes that she has to respond openly and obviously to the feedback she receives, so at the following class meeting she reads the learner comments about one video out loud, without judging the comments or trying to identify the people who called the video "lame" and "boring." This opens up a discussion on what a good video resource might look like, and the learners get excited about the idea of making such a resource for themselves. Susanna feels that she has managed to shift the relationship between herself and the learners just a little bit in a positive direction and looks forward to the next set of learner input.

THE CONTEXT

While many aspects of teaching adults are left to educators, the context in which you are working can make a very significant difference to the way evaluations are conducted and the information is used. However, I think it is useful to be clear that in most settings in which educators work they are interested primarily in the evaluations conducted at the end of a course rather than the ongoing feedback that educators seek as part of their practice. Generally, teachers can seek the insights of learners throughout a course in the ways that they think best, even if, at the end of the course, there is a set of clear formal expectations. Because much of the most useful information for our teaching can come from evaluative activities during the course, this need not be a significant issue for the development and implementation of a system to collect and recognize input.

Organizations that employ educators to work with adults often use evaluation data from students to assess the quality of their teachers' work. In some cases it is the only evidence used to inform these judgments. If the organization is taking this process seriously, there will be a formal system in place to try to ensure some kind of level playing field for the educators, such as a standardized form or a consistent assessment method. It is easy to see why this approach to judging teacher quality is attractive—after all, it is consistent with my main argument here: that learners have a great deal to say about teaching, and that it should be taken into account. Nonetheless, this way of assessing teacher quality must be approached very cautiously.

One major problem is that we do not know what learners see as being good teaching, and we cannot assume that it is the same as the organization's view or the educator's perspective. It will be based on the learning career of the individual learners, which by definition can be highly diverse and varied. More often than not, even organizations that work closely with many educators of adults may not be totally clear on what they regard as high-quality teaching and will use learner evaluations as a pragmatic way to make a judgment. This implies a rather circular definition: something like "good teaching is teaching that gets good evaluations." For educators in a situation where their employment is based on teaching evaluations, it is really important to be clear about how the evaluations will be used. It is essential to know whether a single negative class evaluation will have an impact on the educator's employment, or whether the organization will act on only consistent concerns that are repeated over time. The most reflective organizations will be looking at patterns over time and balancing evaluation feedback with evidence of learning.

Comparability can be an important aspect of evaluation. For example, you might want to try using new resources with one group of learners and compare them with the old materials. In this case, the evaluation really must be consistent across both to be able to make a comparison. Similarly, new educators may be interested in using the same approach as more established ones so that they can assess their areas of development, and any employer that wants to assess teacher quality will want to have consistent tools. The extreme examples are most likely universities, which usually have formal standardized systems that are completed by learners in all classes and become part of the instructors' employment history.

The contexts that use this information most effectively will build professional development around the evaluations. If two or three educators are getting less strong evaluations on a particular area, this can be seen as an opportunity to offer support in that area to all instructors or to set up a peer mentoring system. This creative and supportive use of teaching evaluation is far more reasonable and justifiable than a more judgmental application. In other words, the driving questions should be more like "Where can we improve?" than "Are we doing this well?"

A final note on evaluation concerns the importance of resources. Good evaluation takes time, thought, and materials. It does not emerge automatically. In many settings, the availability of an online evaluation system (at least for end-of-course evaluations) can be very helpful, as it provides both a level of consistency and a degree of anonymity for the learners. In my experience, online systems also boost the response rate from learners to some degree. In contexts with formal evaluation requirements it is well worth considering, and even in less formal contexts an online questionnaire can be a fun and effective way to gather information. This is especially powerful if the participants can write the evaluation survey themselves.

Susanna believes that a method to collect student perspectives should be implemented across the organization, and she presses hard for an anonymous system to be put in place. When this happens, she is surprised to learn that many of the students express their discomfort with the comments and attitudes of other instructors, and some specifically mention Susanna's positive attitude. This is an important lesson for her; it allows her to strengthen her practice without compromising her core beliefs. In addition, the experience underscores the importance of gathering evidence on learner perspectives, and how hard it is for the educator to judge opinions from within the process.

CONCLUSION

When done well, the collection of learners' insights can be an extremely powerful way to improve our teaching. To ensure this, evaluation needs to be credible and clear, with explicit application in the teaching and learning process. Returning to the questions posed at the beginning of the chapter gives rise to the following thoughts:

What insights do learners have into teaching and learning in this setting?

My view is that learners have a great deal of insight, and the more clearly and concretely we ask to hear it, the more useful it will be to us in course design. However, while learners know a lot about their experience of a course and their reaction to it, they may know less about teaching quality and the amount of learning that comes out of a course, so it is important to take comments on these areas seriously but a little cautiously.

What needs to be known about the course?

This will vary depending on the needs of the educator, learners, and the sponsors of the educational activity. For educators the information gathered at the end of the course is useful as a summary, but the more directly applicable insights often come from feedback on specific activities. The two aspects of the course that can be included in evaluation are the general affective and motivational experience of the participants and indications of the effectiveness of concrete procedures. For other stakeholders the question may simply be whether participants see the course as meeting their needs—a broader question that is, unfortunately, harder to answer.

How frequently is input into the course design needed?

The short answer is, as often as possible! Simple, focused, quick evaluations are more useful in helping educators to think about their approach than infrequent long, complex approaches.

Is comparability between different courses needed?

There are specific occasions where comparability is important, such as comparisons between classes. Generally, however, the need for concrete feedback means that most evaluations that we would use in our teaching would be tailored to a specific course with a particular group of learners, suggesting that there will be a fair degree of variability.

Is the focus on learner experience or demonstrated learning?

I believe it is important to be clear on this question—if the information needed is focused on outcomes, this is assessment rather than evaluation. In many contexts this line can be blurred, but as an educator you need to keep these two concepts separate and respond to each appropriately. When learner input is sought, it should be linked to their experience of teaching and learning—the area in which they are the experts.

What sort of resources are available for evaluation?

Evaluation can be very simple, requiring no paper and just five minutes, or it can be a more complex activity. In general, I have found that making an evaluation activity fit the available resources is much better than doing no evaluation at all. For a more complex evaluation—perhaps one that has high stakes for the learners, the educators, or the program—do not underestimate the time required and try to pack it into the last thirty seconds of a class. Ideally, give evaluation activities all the time the learners need.

Understanding learner perspectives on your teaching is a fantastic opportunity to improve your practices and to find out whether your perceptions of the class process are shared. Many times I have looked at evaluation forms only to learn that something I thought was really good was boring for learners, or that something I had made up on the spot in desperation was people's favorite activity of the course! As responsible educators—people who take education seriously— our response to these situations should ideally be interest and application. The mark of great educators is not that they are always right or that they get the best evaluations—rather, it's that they are always learning about themselves and their teaching.

Making Learning Visible

chapter EIGHT

DEMONSTRATING LEARNING

How standardized or individualized?

Are comparable results needed?

What are the external influences?

How detailed does it need to be?

Is there a balance of formative and summative?

How transparent?

Joshua is a former police officer. After a number of years spent working on the streets of the Philadelphia, he left the service and now works as a trainer with a number of police departments. Like many police officers, when Joshua started his career he was rather idealistic, but unlike some he did not become cynical after his experiences. At the end of his career he believed more strongly than ever in community policing—the idea that the police have to work in and with the community rather than try to impose laws heavy-handedly from outside. In fact, the main reason he left the service was that his ideas no longer fit with the philosophy of the city administration, who were intent on following New York's move toward a "tough love," zero-tolerance approach.

Joshua has built up a successful training and consultancy business based on his philosophy of policing. He specializes in working with departments that want to expand their knowledge of less-aggressive models of polic-ing. Inevitably, this means that he is called in when there is a problem in the department (or at least the perception of a problem) and the man-agement wants to respond in some way. He is fairly used to presenting an unpopular way of thinking to officers who are very comfortable with their confrontational methods.

The current contract looks like one of his most challenging ever. He has been contracted by a large Canadian city to work with the police service in the wake of a shooting. The victim was a young man of color whom the police on the scene had assumed was armed, though a gun was never found. The mayor is not supportive of the police service, whom he suspects are hounding and harassing him over his alleged drug use. The police officers are very much in a defensive mode, feeling that they are caught in the middle of several nasty situations, and they are not very open to a fancy consultant coming in to tell them their job.

Joshua suspects that training around issues of ethnicity and racial profil-ing could really help the officers to understand and learn from recent events. The difficulty is not what he should do in the course; he has lots of materials that have worked in the past, and he has had to develop approaches that are effective in the face of defensiveness. The problem is going to be finding out how much, and what, the officers in the course have learned. Given the sensitiveness of the situation, he needs to show that the training has had an effect and changed attitudes. He knows that the officers are smart enough to give him what he wants to see in the assessment, and they probably will. But he wants to really understand the impact of what he is doing and show the officers that they have gained something from the course.

Typically, police training in this city uses multiple-choice exams based on attitude surveys and case studies for assessment, with the "right" answers clearly more correct than the others. Joshua believes that he can do better in his work.

Assessment—finding out what learners have learned—is one of the most challenging aspects of education. It is especially difficult for new educators, who can be uncomfortable with assessing the learning of others, because it feels too much like judging them. All too often, this leads to the imposition of an assessment method that fails to add a great deal to the learning process, and it means the loss of an opportunity to provide useful information to all involved in the teaching and learning process. Despite the educators' hesitancy, learners are usually open to well-designed assessment that gives them information about their progress that they can use in practical ways. Of course, they remain skeptical of assessment methods that do not recognize their intentions and their circumstances.

There has been limited interest in assessment in the tradition of adult education, most likely for three reasons. First, in the past much education for adults has been voluntary, with lots of opportunity for eclectic and voluntary approaches to assessment. And if the focus was more on leisure-related topics, assessment might not be a consideration at all. Second, there was a philosophical belief that education for adults should be distinct from education for children, and choosing not to assess learning was seen as one important way to underline this difference. Third, it was assumed that learning that took place in less formal adult education settings could not transfer to more formal systems, so there was no need for a consistent system to signal achievement and ease transitions. Over the last two or three decades, all three of these reasons have become much less credible, as adult learning has increasingly come to function as a component of a larger system. This has raised interest in assessment as a way to communicate, within and between different types of education, about what people know and can do. If learners are going to study further or move on to a setting such as college, then it is important that they get credit for their existing knowledge.

This chapter covers the following questions:

- How standardized or individualized do assessment approaches need to be?
- To what extent must assessment results be comparable across space and time?
- What external influences on assessment must be recognized?
- How detailed does the information from assessments have to be?
- What sort of balance between formative and summative assessment is desirable?
- Ideally, how transparent should assessment instruments be?

I hope that by the end of the chapter you will have a better sense of the kind of decisions you need to make to be assured that the assessments you use are the most constructive and positive possible. I believe many educators working with adults try to avoid the challenges of assessment. This is really too bad, because it is one of the most useful tools that we have to inform everybody involved in teaching and learning what's been done, how well it's been done, and what needs to be done next. A well-designed assessment should not make learners feel judged; rather, it should help them feel that they have the information they need to make good decisions about their own learning.

COUNTING WHAT COUNTS

Assessment is a complex business, but it is possible to design it well by keeping a small number of relatively intuitive things in mind. At its most straightforward, assessment is about communication. That communication is concerned with what people know about something at different times and the changes that occur in the course of learning. In other words, assessment is communication about learning. Assessment that does not communicate anything to anybody is not very useful. Assessment creates information to be used by somebody in some way. The three most common possible parties to the assessment are the educator, the learners, and an organization (not necessarily the organization hosting the education). Assessment information can have a lot of value for educators, letting them know what has been learned, what remains to be learned, and what parts of the course have been effective. It provides direct feedback on the whole teaching and learning process—learning happens not in a vacuum, but in a complementary relationship with the actions of the educator.

Developing a way to communicate about learning is not always easy. If there is a baseline measure and then a later assessment measure, and if the later assessment shows stronger performance, it is possible to state with some certainty that learning has taken place. The tricky part is knowing exactly what has been learned and why, because assessment is based on sampling what somebody knows (sampling is necessary because assessing everything a person knows is impossible). The design challenge in assessment is finding a way to make the sampling meaningful—even in assessing the most concrete, visible skill, it takes some thought to identify the key elements and how they can be demonstrated.

For learners, assessment information can be enormously reassuring. Done well, assessments can help learners to feel that they are getting somewhere. They can also provide more specific feedback on the details of that progress and point to areas still needing attention and development. In some cases, the information can help learners to select future areas of study or work. I believe strongly that we tend to be good at what genuinely interests us, and looking at how our learning has progressed can help make that clear.

For organizations, assessment may provide evidence that learners have attained a degree of competence in the area of study and are ready to be certified. Beyond this obvious use, assessment information can be applied in a number of further ways. Entry to further study is often based on assessment information, as is allocation of financial support and other resources. Assessment information can be used as a way to assess the quality of an individual teacher's work, though this should be avoided whenever possible because there are so many factors that affect assessment outcomes that are outside the control of the educator.

Overall, assessment is an important focus in teaching that holds a great deal of significance for many people and processes. Educators may want to develop a deeper knowledge than it is possible to cover in this chapter, and they should follow up with further reading (see, for example, Fenwick & Parsons, 2000). As a starting point, however, we can look at a few aspects of assessment that provide a useful framework.

Perhaps the simplest questions, yet one of the most useful, that educators can ask reflects the communicative aspect of assessment—what do we want to know? This is not as obvious as it might seem. We have been trained since our days in school to see assessment as a necessary part of education, something that always happens and that demonstrates that the class is serious. The way that assessment plays its part varies, however, depending on whether the course has specific outcomes. If there is a definite aim for the class, assessment helps us to understand progress toward that goal. In more open situations, some form of assessment could be conducted to find out what people have learned in a general way. There might be no assessment at all, and this could be a perfectly reasonable choice in certain circumstances. The starting point for designing assessment is being absolutely clear about what needs to be known and who needs to know it.

Clear assessment often involves the use of a comparator, something against which performance can be measured. To make this more concrete, we can take the example of learning to cook Indian food. This can be set up as either "Cook a classic Indian curry dish as it is prepared in Mumbai" or "Learn to use Indian spices in a creative and pleasing way." In the first case, assessment is fairly straightforward, as there is clearly something against which our efforts will be judged. In the second case, assessment would be far harder, since what I consider to be a great use of cardamom you might find repulsive. The clearer the comparator for assessment, the more straightforward assessment can be, and if there is no clear comparator, assessment will be of limited value. If the educator wants to know "How are learners enjoying the class?" or "What are they getting out of it?" assessment is not the right approach—these are evaluation questions, as discussed in the previous chapter.

Assuming that we are working in a context where assessment is appropriate and helpful, and we have a clearly identified set of the information we hope to get out of our assessment, the next question is whether we want to use the information formatively or summatively. Formative assessment gives us insights that we use to inform and form the teaching and learning process as we go along. For example, we might learn that nobody in our cooking class seems able to cook garlic in ghee without burning it, so that gives us a really clear indication of something that we should focus on. Summative assessment is the classic end-of-the-class type of test, in which we sum up all the learning that has occurred. For our example, this could be getting everybody to cook butter chicken and getting members of the local community in to rate it for authenticity and taste. It is important to keep these two uses of assessment clearly distinct. Summative assessment really does have to be similar to a demonstration of competence in many cases, whereas formative assessment can be far more open and informal. Even just asking a group of learners questions about the class can count as effective formative assessment.

In recent years there has been increasing emphasis on the use of standardized tests in education, and educators need to decide whether they want to use this type of assessment. The general idea of standardized tests is that the questions are identical so that the results of different people can be compared. This can be really valuable—for example, the educator does things one way one year and somewhat differently the next, and she uses a standardized test so the outcomes of the two methods can be compared. For these results to be absolutely meaningful, however, requires a lot of learners and quite a sophisticated design. More often standardized tests are used in areas where everybody must demonstrate very similar skills, such as a driver's license test.

At the other end of the continuum from standardized tests are highly individualized approaches. Here there is far more room for flexibility, as the aim is not to compare the results of learners against each other, but to get detailed information about the knowledge of a specific person. Asking people to write an essay on a historical event or to prepare their favorite dish using Indian spices are examples of these types of assessments. The actual product of assessment will be quite different for each person, though they may be measured on similar criteria.

Neither of these two approaches is necessarily better. They simply give very different types of information. Typically, more individualized approaches give more diagnostic information, allowing teaching to respond to the specific needs of the learner. It is also possible to follow up and find out why learners gave the response they did, which is much harder with a standardized approach. It can be very useful to have more open-ended types of assessments for formative purposes and more standardized methods for summative purposes.

The type of learning that educators are trying to capture will make a big difference to the assessment approach. Standardized tests are often pen-and-paper tests, typically produced by a testing company. This will not be much use if learners are working on a topic that is either very specialized or very hands-on. You can imagine that a standardized test for car mechanics would give very limited information. In these cases, educators can produce their own simple assessments or the assessment can be very practical. A philosophy of assessment known as "authentic assessment" suggests that the methods used to demonstrate learning should be as close as possible to the way in which the learning will ultimately be used. From this standpoint, the test for transmission rebuilding skills is rebuilding a transmission. This principle can be applied very widely—after all, if you are teaching conversational Greek, should the assessment call for listing verbs or having a conversation in Greek? Assessments can be simple, practical, and very effective.

Different levels of detail are useful in different circumstances. In summative tests it is often enough to show a grasp of the area, whereas formative assessments may need to be more fine-grained to provide detailed information on how the teaching and learning can best proceed. A good rule for assessment is not to gather information that is not going to be used, so be careful about adding more details to an assessment, making it longer and more time-consuming (to take and to review) without adding any value to the activity.

Learners often view "good" assessment results as a reward. Ideally, this aspect of assessments should be downplayed, as their value so often lies in the information they give about ongoing processes rather than the judgment they provide about the quality of the learner's work. However, one positive aspect of this view is that assessment can be used to encourage certain ways of working and approaching tasks. For example, it may be important that learners are prepared for working as part of a team, and in this circumstance it is helpful to set up group activities, with the final assessment outcome shared by all the participants. In this case, assessment models the potential working conditions learners will experience after the course.

The specific methods for assessments are quite flexible and generally can be applied to a range of purposes. For example, a ten-item true/false test can be used as standard summative test to show what everybody knows and how that knowledge compares. Alternatively, it can be used a standard formative test halfway through a course to identify the areas that need more attention. It can be used in an individualized way, to reflect knowledge that you and the learners have agreed they need to know, and the information from this could be used summatively or formatively.

There are many ways to generate and apply assessment information. Here are some of the assessment methods that have I found useful in a range of settings:

- **Journals and diaries.** This involves asking learners to respond briefly to what is going on in class. The assessment concerns the extent to which they are able to draw on their expanding knowledge of the subject area in their response.

- **Role-plays.** Sometimes, when teaching a skill such as customer service, you can ask learners to act out a situation in which they draw on those skills. This may turn into a hilarious exercise, but there will always be a serious core of performance.

- **Group presentations.** A small number of learners can be asked to research a particular topic (or share their own experience of it) with the whole class. This generates new knowledge for the whole class, and it can be assessed for thoroughness and relevance. It's best to avoid assessing the actual presentation and to instead focus on the ideas, as people vary so much in their presentation experience and confidence.

- **Worksheets.** Quick and easy worksheets and quizzes can be fun as long as learners are aware that there isn't too much at stake. Asking people to mark their own can take a lot of the sting out of this type of assessment.

- **Short answer questions.** Asking people to reply in writing to questions like "What are some reasons to be cautious with cardamom?" can be a really useful way to gauge their grasp of a topic. As with presentations, assessment should be based on the ideas and not the presentation, unless the presentation is something they are specifically there to learn.

- **Scenarios.** As with role-plays, scenarios can be a lot of fun for learners without losing their assessment value. They vary from the detailed case studies used in business schools ("You are the CEO of Apple . . .") to very simple situations ("The customer insists on a 10-percent discount . . .") and responses can be oral or in writing.

Once the assessment information is generated, it needs to be given some sort of mark or response. One option that makes sense in many settings is a written response that does not contain any sort of grade or mark, but simply replies to the learner's contribution. This can be truly useful information for the learner, and it takes a lot of pressure out of the situation. At the other end is the percentage or letter grade most of us are familiar with from school. Another version of this is a pass/fail grade or a statement that competencies or outcomes have been achieved or not. When it comes to responding to assessment work, generally the more detail that can be provided and the less judgmental the comments, the better.

The grounds for assessment should not be a surprise for the learners, and one way to ensure this is to give out a rubric, stating clearly what their work will be assessed on, what the expectations are (the comparators), and how marks will be assigned. If the course has formal objectives, the marking expectations should link to these in a clear and unambiguous manner. Learners will be able to use specific feedback to shape their learning far more easily than less focused information.

In the example rubric in Table 8.1, Joshua has started by listing the three aims he hopes to achieve in the course for police officers. He has written them very carefully to be acceptable to the officers in the class without being judgmental in any way. He then completed the column under "strong performance" to describe what he thought would be a good, attainable level of performance. "Very strong performance" is the ideal level he would like people to reach, and "needs work" genuinely reflects a range of approaches that he believes require attention and thought. Although this rubric is clearly specialized (as they all should be—detail is important), the general framework should be clear.

Table 8.1
An Example Rubric

LEARNING OUTCOME	VERY STRONG PERFORMANCE	STRONG PERFORMANCE	NEEDS WORK
Ability to assess risk quickly and accurately	Applies a standard approach, modifying it to fit the circumstances and able to explain those modifications	Applies a standard approach to assessing risk factors	Inconsistent approach, uncertain of priority factors
Demonstration of consistent profession judgment	Anticipates own reactions and plans ways to maintain composure	Aware of own physical reactions to danger and able to set them aside in favor of careful decision making	Believes that risk does not affect decision making and does not prepare for that possibility
Awareness of alternative interventions	Practices and applies a range of different intervention models	Is able to describe a range of alternative, nonviolent intervention approaches to be applied in high-risk situations	Is aware of a small range of options, after which self-defense is necessary

Using a rubric really underlines the communicative value of assessment. It outlines the expectations and provides a form of language to describe the learning that is hoped for. Rubrics should always be shared with learners as early as possible in the course, and developing the rubric with the class, if there is time, is an excellent approach. Assessment must not be secretive, and it should be built on a set of shared values and shared hopes.

Assessment of learning is a key aspect of design, but it has to be approached in a respectful and appropriate way. The starting point remains the question of what needs to be known and by whom; from there, the next questions concern the use to which this information will be put. Of course, the potentially perfect assessment tool is not always available, due to the constraints and expectations of real-life programs, discussed in the following sections.

THE EDUCATOR

Because assessment is seen as a bit mysterious, it's very common for new educators to assess learners using the same approaches that were used on them when they were learners. This approach can lead to using high-stakes forms of assessments (such as tests and examinations) in situations where there are more appropriate and constructive options. I believe that if educators can think more about the purposes of assessment, then they can perhaps avoid using a method that is less useful to themselves and the learners than they hope.

The primary use for assessment information from the educator's point of view is to help with planning and delivering instruction, which implies that formative assessment methods are extremely significant. It can be helpful to begin formative assessment very early in the course, and if you want to have a baseline measure of learners' starting points, it has to be established at the beginning so you can gain a picture of learning over the whole course. Baseline measures, and formative evaluation generally, do not have to be extremely formal. A quick and fun quiz asking people a series of questions about the topic will work well. Their responses can be reviewed by the educator and returned to the learners. At the end of the course the same quiz can be completed again and marked by the whole class together. This gives learners a real sense of accomplishment and bookends the course nicely. If the course runs over a number of weeks, it is not unreasonable to have several such assessments.

Any assessment that is going to be used for diagnosis and formative purposes needs to have good discriminatory power. This means that it should provide enough information to allow for instructional judgments to be made. Suppose, for example, that the course is bookkeeping and the educator wants a clear starting point for teaching. It is not very helpful if there is a brief test on accountancy that finds that the learners are not very good at bookkeeping. They know that; that's why they are in the course! What is needed for teaching is an insight into the specifics of what people can do and cannot do. It's important that formative assessments indicate the details of where the focus of the class needs to be placed.

Related to this, it's important that assessment be clear to all involved, in terms of what is being asked and the reasons for asking it. This includes the educator, who needs to be able to easily and quickly draw implications for teaching from the assessment outcomes.

It is useful for the educator to consider what sort of behaviors are encouraged by a good mark on assessment (if it is being given a mark). This is where the assessment methods really come together with the teaching approaches. However much the learners are told that they should work together in the course, if they are being given individual marks, this will undermine collective approaches and inevitably create caution about sharing ideas and resources. The messages given by assessment can be very powerful and hard to contradict.

All of this can make it sound as if assessment is extremely hard to get right, but it really is not. Assessment is fairly straightforward as long as educators know what they want out of it, and most often this will tend to point toward less complicated, less formal forms of assessment. Even though we have been conditioned to think of assessment in a particular way throughout our educational career—usually as a zero sum game with high stakes attached—there is no reason why our own educational practices have to continue this emphasis.

Thinking about assessment as a way to generate information that supports learning can help educators to move beyond "testing." The metaphor I like to use instead is mapping. Assessment is a process of taking sightings to work out what point we have reached and the direction in which we should continue, helping us to work out which path we should follow and for how long.

Before we leave educators' views of assessment, it is worth recognizing that some teachers of adults are very skeptical about assessment, which they see as a form of power being exercised over learners. There is no denying it can be used in this way—or rather, misused. It is possible in certain circumstances for educators to use the threat of a bad mark, whether implicit or explicit, as a tool in classroom management. I consider this to be a mark of inappropriate teaching. I believe that we educators who have chosen to work with adults have also chosen to take on a moral responsibility to build a positive and collective learning environment that values the learning careers of all the learners, whatever stage they may be at. Bad or clumsy assessment can undermine this possibility. Applied well, assessment can ensure that this responsibility is met.

Joshua is torn. On the one hand, it is clear that the police officers do have a lot to learn. On the other, he will lose all credibility if he tries to come in as an outsider and tell them what they need to know. He decides to establish a baseline measure based on a scenario where the participants have to describe and talk through alternative responses. This will allow him to not only get a feel for what the groups know about different approaches but also see what their reactions are when confronted with more unusual ideas. He decides to begin the training session with thirty minutes dedicated to this activity.

THE LEARNERS

For most learners, most of the time, the question they want to have answered through assessment is "How am I doing?" This would seem to suggest that learners would welcome assessments of various types, but in my experience learners are often cautious about assessment. The most likely explanation for this, in my view, is that their learning careers have not been marked by careful and responsible uses of assessment—for most of us, assessment has traditionally meant closed-book tests, with our responses allocated marks that are made public and have repercussions for our future choices. Although this may make sense for school students (though this is debated by many educators), it is rarely appropriate for adults. Learners who remember this type of assessment and view it as the only option will understandably be concerned.

Throughout the history of adult education, the learners have tended to be those who have not done well in school. This is no longer the case; there is a clear trend to encourage younger and more educated people to participate in adult learning (see UK data, Mason, 2010). These new types of learners, who may be coming to adult learning with a career of educational success behind them, are less likely to be worried about assessment.

The philosophy of assessment in adult learning finds itself very much in line with the field of universal design (Burgstahler, 2012). Assessment techniques, irrespective of the details, are not neutral. They are easier or more challenging depending on the cultural background of the learner, their experience, and how easy they find it to learn in a certain area and through a certain method. It matters very much that a person is a second language learner, or that a person has grown up dealing with poverty, or that it may take a person a while to write out responses to questions. None of these factors has much to do with what people learn, but they all affect how people can *show* what they have learned. It is important for educators of adults to give the widest possible range of learners an opportunity to demonstrate their attainment—so if assessments are to achieve this, they must not be implicitly more difficult for some groups than others. An excellent resource to start your exploration of universal design is available from the Teacher Excellence in Adult Literacy Center (listed in Appendix B).

The best way to know the views of learners regarding assessment is to ask them to help design the assessments. Very rarely do adult learners try to find an easy option for themselves, despite new educators' concern that they might. Generally they will consider the alternatives and be very straightforward about what they believe will be effective assessment. The educator can take their views into account in a number of ways. One relatively straightforward approach is to offer choices of assessment method at each stage of a course. This is more work for the educator, but may provide far more useful information about the learning that is taking place than a universal approach that nobody likes or believes in.

For assessment to make sense to learners, there needs to be a clear rationale for it. Most people do not like assessment very much, yet we are asking learners to participate in it, and it seems respectful to explain why they should consider it. If there is no clear rationale for it, assessment is not good practice in and of itself. Good practice starts with being able to explain what assessment is for, why it's helpful, and the use the educator can make of the information. If it's not possible to explain clearly and simply what it is for, then it may be best not to assess formally at all.

Some learners will talk about having test anxiety and make an argument that they should not be assessed. This is a tricky situation to handle, especially where there are clear expectations that learning will be assessed. I view test anxiety as a product of accumulated bad experiences, and I sometimes find it is possible to work with a number of low-stakes, simple tests to build credibility and confidence in the assessment process. If the course is leading to a specific final assessment, practice runs through the test can be helpful, but it is important to ensure that the messages from these assessments are kept positive.

Just like educators, learners are often far more interested in formative assessment than in summative. As partners in the teaching and learning process, they appreciate guidance on what is going well and where their efforts should be concentrated. Frequent low-stakes assessment can work very well for these purposes, providing useful information to everybody involved while not causing much anxiety. They can usefully be varied, with a mixture of brief tests, short answer format, and group assessments.

Some adult learners are interested in the final mark, if it's that kind of course, but many are very pragmatic about it and simply want to make sure they can move on to the next thing they want to learn or do. As a learner I strongly prefer pass/fail assessments, not because I don't do reasonably well on graded tests but because grades do not motivate me at all. All I care about is the pragmatic question of whether I can progress. Pass/fail approaches to summative assessment can be a good option in situations where final assessment is necessary but the format is left open.

One interesting approach to summative evaluation is to have a number of assessments spread throughout a course and then allow the learners to choose the ones they want to combine into the final assessment mark. So there may be assessments such as:

1. Presentation on the history of policing: 25 percent

2. Review of three alternative interventions: 25 percent

3. Presentation of a specific case study: 25 percent

4. Production of a two-minute video scenario: 25 percent

5. Written document analyzing city policy on weapon use: 25 percent

Learners choose which four of these five activities they would like to contribute to the final outcome, depending on the types of activities they are most comfortable with. A responsible educator will develop a range of assessments to take into account the specific needs of the learners.

Typically, of course, folks will choose the assessments they did best in, but this is not a problem—the idea is to allow people to demonstrate their learning to its best advantage, and it helps people to feel that everything is not on the line every time they complete an assessment. Very often, assessments designed in this way can provide formative information as well as contributing to a summative outcome.

In my experience, we can summarize the views of learners quite intuitively. To have credibility with learners, assessment has to be meaningful and useful, meaning that there must be clarity about the purposes and about the information gathered. Generally, formative assessments and approaches that gather data "little and often" are preferred. Assessment should be built into the process of the course, not stuck on in an awkward way. Learners may be skeptical about assessment, but if it has a clear purpose they will often be happy to participate in designing it, making sure it fits their learning needs and informs teaching.

Joshua knows that the police officers are busy people and do not want to feel they are wasting their time, so he ensures that evaluation is tied to goals that make sense for the participants. In choosing ways for them to demonstrate competence, he focuses on practical actions; the last thing members of the police need is more paperwork. In every way, he works to link assessment—and demonstration—of learning to the concrete realities of the officers' work.

THE CONTEXT

While there is often a high degree of consistency between the perspectives on educators and learners on assessment, contextual factors may pull in a very different direction. The first point to make is that in many cases formative assessment is of little interest to the organization. Because the information produced is focused on the teaching and learning process, it may not be very useful beyond the participants in that process. It is not atypical for educators to have almost complete freedom with regard to formative assessment, as they do with teaching practices, but this is far less often the case with summative assessment.

A very obvious example of this situation is when the course leads to some form of certification. Here the emphasis is almost always on summative results—for example, do the learners know what they are expected to know to be considered as a qualified plumber? Can they carry out the tasks required of them in their employment? In some cases these requirements come from within the organization sponsoring and delivering the teaching, but in an increasing number of cases there is an external organization that certifies learners as having met the required standards. This raises questions about who actually designs, implements, and marks the assessments—it may be not the educator but somebody completely outside the situation.

Organizations may consider the assessment outcomes as a measure of the quality of the education taking place in the classroom, and therefore of the teacher. This is a problem for a number of reasons. There is a huge range of factors that affect the outcome of educational processes, and most of them are beyond the educator's control. To take two examples, the starting point and the motivations of the learners may be very different. In a class of adult learners some may have learning careers that have been very successful and very formal; others may have finished an unhappy school career thirty years before. In a course that leads to marks, the first group will have a huge advantage, not least because they have had more practice with assessments. Similarly, some learners may be in class just to get through, while others may have a really competitive attitude and want to get the highest marks possible. Very few assessment systems are sensitive enough to capture all of this variety, and the students' final attainment does not really tell us a lot about the teaching and learning process in all its variations.

There may be an argument for tying assessment to teaching quality when the test is an external one and the educator's focus is on supporting motivated learners to pass it. The example that comes to mind is driving instruction. Not everybody will pass the driver's test—nor should they—but a good instructor will get the maximum possible number of candidates up to the required standard. Beyond this very crude sort of indicator, extreme care should be taken with connecting instructor quality and assessment outcomes, or even the work of the organization and outcomes. One unintended effect of making this sort of connection is "cream skimming," in which courses recruit the best potential students to make sure their results look good. This is clearly an ethical problem!

There are a couple of pragmatic aspects of assessment in which organizations have an interest. These include the cost. As with any activity that takes time and resources, assessment is not free. The minimum cost is the many instructor hours it takes to develop and respond to assessment; in addition, the tests or other methods may have a cost per unit. This underlines once more the need for assessments to have a clear purpose and value, and for them to generate information that communicates meaningfully to as many people as possible.

Organizations have a preference for assessments that are cumulative and systematic. This means that they build on one another in a way that makes sense. If one class deals with law for house buyers, for example, and the other deals with law for house sellers, then the assessment areas will fit together in a complementary way. The types of assessments will ideally be similar, so that all involved end up with a coherent picture of the knowledge that has come out of the classes. It is also important to include anything that learners need to know so as to be able to progress to a later stage of learning.

When it comes to assessment, contextual factors generally push toward rigorous summative assessment, but this does not mean it is the only option. Once again, decisions should reflect the uses of the information that assessment generates and how it adds value to the teaching and learning process.

Joshua finds that the expectations of the police force do require competence statements to come out of the training provided by consultants. He understands this completely, but in his work he believes that he needs the freedom to reflect the interests of the participants. To address both sides of the issue, he adds a first learning outcome to his aims: "To identify critical issues affecting the performance of police officers." In this way, the opening conversations and explorations of current concerns become part of the content of the course, and assessment can give value to the officers' own knowledge of their situation.

CONCLUSION

Assessment is a controversial area when it comes to the teaching of adults. Many people have very strong convictions and philosophies about it; some believe in the results of strong, rigorous assessment as essential data, others are very cautious about it. The position that seems to be most useful is to recognize the complexity of assessment and make informed decisions about the type and extent of assessment.

Repeatedly in our discussion of assessment I have suggested that you need to understand two things when designing assessment: what you need to know, and how this will add to the teaching and learning process. Assessment is a communicative process, and the helpfulness of that communication has to be the key concern. In that light, we can now return to the central questions of the chapter.

How standardized or individualized do assessment approaches need to be?

Educators and learners tend to prefer more individualized types of assessment that provide instructionally valuable information, but this is balanced in some contexts by a need for standard, or at least comparable, information. It may be best to have a mix, with lots of low-stakes, individualized, formative assessments for the purpose of instruction and a final standardized summative assessment if that fits the requirements of the context.

To what extent must assessment results be comparable across space and time?

The more necessary it is for assessment outcomes to communicate across groups, the more comparable the information needs to be. If this is the case, even individualized assessments should build toward a an overall framework that can be used in other classes at the same time or in subsequent courses.

What external influences on assessment must be recognized?

If the course is building toward certification, or if the organization housing the course has established practices, there is often little freedom regarding the assessment choices that need to be made. External influences need to be respected, though the way that the educator works within the class to meet external expectations can vary considerably; this allows for both learner and educator perspectives to be acknowledged.

How detailed does the information from assessments have to be?

For formative evaluation especially, fairly detailed information can be really helpful in planning instruction and further learning. In general, summative evaluation can be less detailed, as it is built on the principle of sampling people's knowledge rather than capturing it all. More information and detail comes at the cost of time and goodwill, so it makes a lot of sense to aim for a level of detail that provides the necessary information without overwhelming all involved.

What sort of balance between formative and summative assessment is desirable?

Ideally, there will be as much formative assessment as possible, as it provides direct instructional guidance, but the potential need for summative methods should not be overlooked. A balance that swings too far toward summative assessment should be avoided in education, not only with adults but generally, as it can create a highly judgmental context that may be viewed as unsupportive by learners.

Ideally, how transparent should assessment instruments be?

For most purposes, it makes sense to have transparent assessments. Education is one of the few settings in life in which we are asked to respond to a situation with no external resources and little support. More authentic forms of assessment that actually come closer to representing real-life challenges are generally far more open in their approach, and they clearly inform the people being assessed what will be expected and why. This is one of the great values of rubrics and marking schemes that are distributed in advance—they communicate expectations to all involved.

In assessment, less is more. The wise selection of the right method guarantees that valuable information will be generated for teaching and learning, as well as ensuring that the course has provided learners with what they need to learn and to progress.

chapter NINE

You Can Take It with You!

LEARNING TRANSFER

What sort of transfer is possible?

What is the boundary for transfer?

How can it be demonstrated?

What are viable strategies to support transfer?

What are expectations of transfer?

How can educator influence transfer?

What if you put on a terrific course and it changes nothing? What if people come, enjoy a couple of days of training, agree it's important, and then go home and do the same things they did before? That's the worry that haunts Allyson. Working as a nurse-educator for a teaching hospital, she knows that doing things differently can make a real difference to the health outcomes for patients. But she also knows that the environment for the nurses encourages them to continue doing the same things the same way they have traditionally been done. Doctors are still the most powerful people in many wards, and they have come to expect nurses to behave in a particular way.

This is especially true for Allyson's current project. She has developed a course on physician-nurse-tech care teams. In these teams, the different members come together to provide seamless care to the patient, making collective care decisions based on their combined expertise. Allyson strongly believes in this approach, and she is committed to the idea that it leads to better care and stronger relationships between the different members of the team. Diagnoses and treatment tend to be quicker and more accurate, and treatment problems far less frequent. Overall, Allyson sees it as a major step forward for health care.

However, she knows that not everybody feels that way, and that this idea will need to be implemented one step at a time. The starting point has to be informing people about the approach. As a nurse-educator, she has the opportunity to talk with hundreds of people a year, exposing them to the new ideas and spending time working through the benefits and challenges. Yet she knows that there is some reluctance to move to a care team approach, and she has heard from people who work with her former students that very often the training is not implemented. Even when it comes to the most concrete and helpful changes, people do not put them into place for very long, if at all. It seems that there is a high degree of inertia in health care settings, meaning that people find it much easier to keep doing what they have been doing.

Allyson is not sure where the inertia comes from. The nurses she works with blame the doctors; the doctors sometimes accuse the nursing staff of refusing to adopt new ideas. Allyson has decided to start very simply with her students, giving them the evidence that care teams work, and asking them to start working more closely with techs. She hopes that other staff will see the effects of these collaborations and the ideas will spread. Allyson knows, however, that although she can give the nurses lots of support, they will have to implement the ideas in their own institutions.

Allyson knows that she can't *make* people adopt new practices in their work. But she is sure that there must be ways she can approach her teaching that make it more likely. Now she just has to work out what those might be.

For many educational programs working with adults, transfer of learning is the most important outcome. The whole point of the enterprise is that participants will take what they have learned in the course and apply it. For example, a short program on handling forklift trucks safely in a warehouse is really worth giving only if the learners can return to their jobs and behave in a way that results in fewer accidents. This aspect of designing programs has received little attention from most of the people writing about the education of adults (Sork, 2010). Honorable exceptions include Rosemary Caffarella (2002), whose program planning model underlines the importance of transfer of learning, and Daffron and North (2011), who have produced a very useful book dedicated to questions of learning transfer. Luckily, human resource development and training literature contains a lot of discussion on transfer, and we can gain a great deal of insight from this work.

As designers of educational programs, educators stand to benefit from careful thought about transfer of learning, as do the program participants and other stakeholders. This applies in academic areas as well as work-centered contexts. Even a theoretical course can benefit from consideration of what learners are expected to do with their new knowledge.

In this chapter, I will look at the following questions:

- What sort of transfer is possible?
- What is the boundary for transfer?
- How can transfer of learning be demonstrated?
- What are the viable strategies to support transfer?
- What are the expectations of transfer?
- What opportunities does the educator have to influence transfer?

Effective transfer of learning has both technical and affective aspects. There is no silver bullet, no guaranteed way of designing a program that ensures that participants will apply what they learn. But we educators can do a number of things to increase the likelihood that the knowledge we create in our programs both is useful and will be used. If learners decide that they are not going to adopt the ways of thinking and acting that we explain in our teaching, there is not a lot we can do about it. As with so many aspects of education for adults, the key considerations are the motivation and engagement of the learners.

Transfer is often the most important demonstration of the value of our programs. By showing that people have a new way to do things, that they have added a new string to their bow, we can argue that they have increased capacity. This concept, and this argument, is a powerful and effective way to capture the value of much of our work.

MOVING LEARNING BEYOND THE COURSE

Transfer of learning is concerned with the extent to which people actually apply what they learn. It is an interesting area because it is easy to assume that the progression is always strictly logical: we take the course and *then* we find out if we can transfer the new knowledge. This is a bit misleading. What seems to happen is that people evaluate the course while they are in it by asking whether the knowledge they are gaining will be of any use to them once the course is over. This concern is what drives children to ask "But how will I actually use calculus once I have left school?" and leaves parents desperately looking for an answer that isn't to do with the speed of a ball at the top of a throw. In the case of adult learners, we can hope to be a little more prepared to answer this unspoken question, because it does affect the credibility of our programs.

As a concrete example of what we mean when we talk about transfer, I will use a serious, real-life example. Captains and crew of fishing boats in Canada have to go through a lot of training to get a license. Part of the training—perhaps the most important part—concerns safety. They are taught the importance of emergency beacons, life jackets (now called personal flotation devices or PFDs), and careful attention to weather reports. However, research into fishing accidents, many of them very serious, shows that the fishers do not follow what they are taught (Boshier, 2000). They head off into bad weather with no emergency gear and the crew not wearing PFDs. The reasons vary, including a very strong culture of superstition and macho attitudes in the fishing industry and some physical awkwardness associated with wearing the safety gear. Yet time after time, safety reports after fatal incidents show that if the fishers who lost their lives had transferred the learning from their compulsory courses to their everyday practices, many of them would have survived. The conclusion that comes out of this and similar studies is that transfer of learning does not come entirely from rationality; cultural and social aspects have to be taken into account.

The same insights apply in many different fields, such as health. It is really hard to change your behavior as the result of new information. We have known for fifty years that cigarettes have major health consequences, yet people still continue to smoke and, perhaps even more puzzling, to start smoking. One great contribution to understanding this phenomenon is the social learning theory referred to earlier (Bandura, 2004). This work points out that to make a change, the individual has to believe that he is capable of making the change, and this belief is not only individual but social. If I decide I want to give up bacon to improve my health, for example, this has repercussions beyond my own behavior. My family has to support the decision and not expect me to fail, and maybe even consider changing their own practices—no more watching TV with a huge bowl of crispy bacon being passed around (I should add that this isn't a real example). The point is that changes in the way we do things are rarely easy and rarely affect only ourselves; they have to fit with our environment in some way. As long as adolescents think that the danger of cigarettes is both distant and alluring, they will begin smoking.

If we bring this back to transfer of learning, there are clearly some aspects of course design we can control and some we cannot. The wisest approach for educators is to ensure that they do a good job with the factors they can realistically influence and not aim for 100-percent transfer in every program. To some extent, people will always take what they need or want from classes, and our job is to provide a range of knowledge that may be more or less useful for each learner. However, as there is some possibility that our programs will be evaluated for the demonstrated transfer, it is essential to ensure that we do understand the expectations and have a plan to meet them.

I will discuss three aspects of transfer that I think are particularly useful to think about. The first is the disposition of the learners or the way they approach the course (Ottoson, 1997). Following from the earlier discussion of the need for adults to have a reason to learn something, it perhaps is not surprising that they are also more likely to transfer what they learn if they come into the course with the expectation that it will help them with a problem. The other side, of course, is that if they are present without believing there is any real reason to be there (including intrinsic reasons like genuine interest), the transfer of learning will be far more limited. It makes sense that if people are not motivated to learn they will not have anything to apply.

This may seem relatively easy to deal with, but we should not underrate the power of the "need to know." In the fishing example, the people attending the training had a need to know that extended only as far as was necessary to get the license. So despite overwhelming evidence that certain behaviors and choices could save many lives, the transfer between reading that in a book and changing shipboard practices did not happen, not least because in commercial fishing culture the risks were already covered by the superstitious practices. In the minds of the learners there often was no problem to solve. The disposition of the learners can be either a powerful support for transfer of learning or an almost insurmountable barrier.

This brings our discussion back to some of the strategies discussed earlier in the book for building opportunities to work with learners in designing the course. These approaches could potentially work to enhance transfer of learning as well, by helping the educator start from problems that learners see as important. Any strategy that can tie the course back to the real-life concerns of learners is likely to make transfer more probable and more substantial.

Another aspect of transfer is sometimes referred to using the technical term "isomorphism" (Kaminsky, Sloutsky, & Heckler, 2005). In more familiar language, this means the situation in which we learn something is similar to the one in which we apply it. So, for example, in learning French for a trip to Paris, one effective way to prepare would be to practice ordering dinner while being stared at pityingly by a French-speaking waitperson. The issue of isomorphism, or a lack of it, is more significant than people who are not educators might think. When we teach something, we very rarely do so "on the job" in the full sense of the term. We teach in a special place dedicated to teaching, with all the conditions that entails. The knowledge that we teach is abstracted and removed from the context, even with the best will in the world to limit abstraction and keep things concrete. So isomorphism can be a tricky goal to aim for.

One way to arrange teaching to recognize the potential value of isomorphism is to tie teaching very strongly to the concrete skills and tasks that you hope people can manage by the end of the course. This is a double-edged strategy. There is no doubt that making things very concrete can help people to learn. But it also can make it harder to adapt that learning to a new situation because they cannot abstract what they have learned and reformulate it to fit the novel circumstances (Kaminsky, Sloutsky & Heckler, 2005). An example would be if I learned that screw-in lightbulbs unscrew counterclockwise and tighten in the opposite direction. Then I have to unscrew a bolt on my bicycle and am not sure which direction to turn. Because I have learned about lightbulbs concretely, I may not have the abstract knowledge that almost all screw threads in the world work in the same direction.

In the case of the fishers, there is a very significant lack of isomorphism. They are reading in a book that, for example, 78 percent of crewmembers lost in the Strait of Georgia were not wearing PFDs. The behavioral outcome the educators are hoping for is that these fishers will then go out and wear their PFDs and insist that their colleagues do too. This is a huge leap from abstract to concrete. What was needed instead was a way to ensure that the crew do not feel normal without their PFDs, as most of us now feel about seatbelts. The latter feeling, in my case, came from being legally required to wear a seatbelt when I started driving, so it very quickly became part of the routine. The challenge for the educators working with the fishing crews is finding a way to instill donning a PFD as part of the routine, everyday life of working on a fishing boat. The current approach of lecture and appeal to rationality is unlikely to succeed to any real extent.

The final aspect I'll discuss here is the educator's understanding of the context of application. It is generally accepted that transfer from course to application is deeply contextual and must not be treated simply as a technical exercise (Merriam & Leahy, 2005). The way that people around the learners will receive the ideas they learned on a course when they get back to work, the strength of existing practices, and their energy and interest in change all vary a great deal and all make a difference. It may be easy, and the learner can apply what she learned in a straightforward way with no barriers, or it may be that there is a lot of hard work to be done. In any case, the experts on this process will be the learners, not the educators. It is helpful to understand a little about the context of application, but in the end it is the learners who will have to make it work.

The ideas I've discussed here—disposition, isomorphism, and understanding the context—are central aspects of the theory called "experiential learning." This approach to learning starts from the premise that all human learning comes from experience, and it tries to understand more about how that works. The best-known approach is Kolb's Learning Cycle (Kolb, 1984). Learners have an experience, they reflect on it, they draw conclusions, and then, based on these conclusions, they make plans for the next time they perform the action. One way to achieve good learning transfer is to use an educational process for the reflection, analysis, and planning steps. So, for example, a nurse might try to move toward a team approach, experience some difficulty, have an opportunity to reflect on this in professional development, and then return to the work context with new strategies to apply.

Taylor (1997) offers ways to link learning experiences to the contexts in which new knowledge should be used, proposing that application exercises should be built into courses. Going further, he also suggests that learners work together to build transfer strategies—that is, plans for how they can actually implement some of the new perspectives they are learning. This is an interesting idea, with the potential to increase engagement by recognizing learner expertise as well as coming up with concrete actions to be taken. It can be built around scenarios, themselves learner-generated, such as "If there is no resource support for doing things differently, how can changes be put into place without cost?"

In the fisher example, there was no discussion in the safety course of how the knowledge gained could be applied back on the boat, nor any recognition of the macho culture of the boats and suggestions for how safety concerns could be talked about in this context. There was an opportunity for the people taking the course to look at ways to support safe practices that would make sense to a fisher with thirty years of experience, but this was overlooked. As mentioned in Chapter Two, the experience of older learners is too valuable to be ignored. In this case, however, the expertise of the people in the room was neglected, rather than being put into the service of the course and the intended outcomes. The same thing applies in the case of Allyson's course, where she had not yet found a way to harness the expertise of the participants to address the possibility of changing the workplace.

When we think about transfer of learning, we are really trying to think about ways to make the wall between the classroom and real life more transparent and porous. Ideally, we want learners to gain knowledge that they can see the use for, that recognizes the context of their lives outside the classroom and links the course content to that context. As with a number of other areas in this book, the learners themselves can help the educator to complete these tasks successfully and to raise the effectiveness of teaching and learning.

THE EDUCATOR

The educator's approach to the transfer of learning will depend on a number of factors, some more philosophical and some more pragmatic. There is a possibility that the educator is not interested in application as an outcome of the course they are delivering. This is a perfectly reasonable position to take. However, it may be that the educator is seeing transfer and application in a particular, narrow way, and if she took a different view of transfer of learning she could consider application in her design. For people who are teaching practical subjects, application may appear straightforward; for courses in something more esoteric, the concept is admittedly more challenging. It can really help to remember that application of what is learned will look radically different according to the circumstances.

One interesting exercise really brought this home to me. The people running arts programs at a university were asked to talk about the uses of a degree in art history. This is the degree that seems to be pointed to most often as both an easy option and a shortcut to a job in fast food. The faculty came up with a long list of skills—such as attention to detail, ability to analyze individual features alongside the big picture, and organization of work effort—that were enormously practical and very relevant to the sorts of abilities employers say they are looking for. Based on this, they were able to make the claim that art history was actually one of the most practical degrees you could have. The same sort of exercise can help educators to see their subjects in a new way and to identify some of the deeper areas of transferable learning that can be so valuable for learners.

The educator's own experience with transfer of learning can inform his thinking about how it can be achieved and demonstrated in his course. I once knew an educator who was qualified as a commercial chef, which is a trade with an apprenticeship. He then moved on to become an instructor in trades training programs, and the learners he worked with loved him because he was so clear, organized, and systematic—all attributes that transferred from his initial training in kitchen management. This educator both understood learning transfer and worked hard at making it a reality.

Based on their view of the importance of transfer, educators can choose to devote more time to transfer preparation activities and to make it a central aspect of course design. This could also include thinking about the degree to which the course should be isomorphic with the context of application. There is huge potential in this idea for creating interesting courses. A few years ago I studied outdoor education (in Scotland, where the main thing to learn is how to keep dry). Outdoor education has taken the principle of isomorphism very seriously. If you are working with a group of administrators and want to help them to think about ways to simplify bureaucratic procedures, you might ask them to move a twelve-foot plank through a web of ropes, for example. In the debrief session, the topic can move from which ropes they would like to cut to make their task easier to which procedures are the most difficult for them in their working life. There is an isomorphism between the tangled ropes and the tangles of their work.

If educators decide that they want to place transfer at the center of their courses, it can be really helpful to have good knowledge of the context of application—what kind of environment will these folks return to after the course? As social learning theory suggests, a course on healthy eating will have little effect if the learners work in an environment that makes unhealthy snacking easy. If the educator knows that this kind of barrier exists, it becomes far easier to support transfer by designing parts of the course to focus on ways to overcome them. If the educator is less familiar with the context, working with the learners to understand the potential for transfer can be extremely useful.

One way to underline the place of application in the course is to ensure that there is an objective or outcome for the course, something like "Learners will develop a plan for implementing what they learn in this course." This really encourages learners to think about which bits of what they have learned will be useful and how they can be used.

It can be a valuable exercise for educators to think about transfer of learning even if they are a little doubtful about how realistic this possibility is. It can help a great deal with "sharpening up" the aims of the course and can provide a way to talk knowledgeably about the potential value of the course for learners.

Allyson realizes the main problem she is facing in supporting the spread of team approaches to health care is the transfer of learning. She believes she understands the context for application of the knowledge quite well, and she knows from student input that the idea appeals very strongly to the program participants. It seems to her that perhaps the challenge she must find a way to deal with is that of isomorphism—making the content of her courses reflect more accurately the opportunities and challenges of hospital work.

THE LEARNERS

We should never forget that the people who actually do the work of making learning transfer happen are the learners. First, we need to acknowledge that learners will transfer learning only if they are engaged in the course. If they are less engaged, they will learn less, and not only will they have less to transfer, but they may also be less interested in transferring what they have learned. The degree to which the course responds to learner needs and interests in the here and now affects the degree to which the course will have a longer-term impact on the participants.

One central principle to bring about engagement, mentioned earlier, is to ensure that the course you are providing responds to a problem that learners are likely to think needs to be addressed. Sometimes you know in advance what the problems are, but quite often only when the course begins and you meet the learners can you get a real sense of what they see as critical. It's not unusual for an educator to be asked to provide a session on a new software system, only to turn up on the day and find that the participants' perceived problem is that the company keeps changing how it wants things done. It can enhance your teaching and its longer-term effects a great deal if you can find a way to learn something about the likely perceptions of the learners beforehand—while you are designing the course.

It will also make a difference if the learners have the level of self-efficacy necessary to believe that they can make a change by transferring their learning. Even people who start with a high level of self-efficacy can have it eroded over the years. People who work for big companies can find that they learn new procedures in a great staff development program and then return to work only to find it impossible to implement those ideas. If this happens time and time again, their belief in the ability to apply learning will, not unnaturally, be reduced.

The same consideration can also reflect a learner's learning career. If her history as a learner is to engage with a topic, learn all about it, and then not get a good mark because she doesn't "test well," the overall effect may well be to undermine her self-efficacy as a learner and, by extension, as a person who applies learning. Doing things differently, whether in personal or professional life, is always a bit of a risk, and lack of success can make it feel even more risky. Planning for transfer and giving lots of positive reinforcement for taking risks in the class can really pay off.

The insider knowledge of participants coming out of a particular context, attending the course, and then returning to the same context should not be overlooked. It is a wonderful resource for the educator, and, of equal value, their knowledge can serve as a resource for each other. A group of people who share a work context in which they will apply what they are learning can find a real source of power in coming together to discuss how they can use what they have learned. The educator's role is to work with people to develop options and approaches that they hadn't thought of and that might be effective options for application. Part of that process is building an awareness of when people are being realistic in their concerns and when they are overemphasizing difficulties.

The educator should never lose sight of the key role that participants play in making transfer of learning happen. This is not an outcome that the educator can guarantee—after all, transfer of learning often requires some sort of change, and change is always difficult. However, by raising learners' awareness of application and its challenges, educators can make the issue explicit and get ideas from the people who are most likely to know how to make it work. I like the idea of transfer as the outcome of a partnership of learners and educators, wherein the learners benefit by having an opportunity to learn things that will be really useful to them, and educators get to work more directly with the expectations and lived experience of participants.

As Allyson thinks more about isomorphism, she starts to wonder if perhaps she could have used the knowledge of the learners more. Could they be the ones to map their work context and plan ways to deal with it in professional development? Based on what she knows about experiential learning, she realizes that this could be a very powerful way to bring the learning more into line with learners' experience, and it could make transfer far stronger. She needs to put the lived experiences of participants at the center of her work.

THE CONTEXT

When we think about transfer of learning, there are really two contexts to take into account—the context in which things are being learned and the context in which we hope they are being applied. This is always true, whether the contexts are a classroom and a workplace or a computer and a living room. In some ways the process of learning can be considered as the development of ways to move knowledge around between these contexts.

The different forms these contexts can take matters, as does the relationship between them. This relationship can, for example, be very formal, wherein people learn in lectures, pass exams, get certified, and then are expected to be able to do certain things in a particular context. It can also be far more informal, such as when I learn a new word in French from a family member and then use it in an email to a friend. The difference between these two different types of relationships is reflected in different expectations for transfer and the way that it will be demonstrated.

In the first, more formal, case, transfer of knowledge is the point of the whole system, and it is likely to be monitored and evaluated. Not so in the second case. For most of us working as educators of adults, the relationship between contexts will be somewhere in the middle, with some expectations for transfer and a degree of monitoring of transfer (though it usually is not talked about in those terms). For example, when I was teaching in employment preparation programs, the two contexts were somewhat linked. We tried to have work-like expectations for dress and conduct in the classroom, and we knew whether that knowledge was transferred by participants because it contributed to their becoming employed.

Educators need to know what this relationship is like, and the place to start is by looking at the orientation to application within the teaching organization. There can be a direct link, with the organization guaranteeing that people will learn everything they need to be a successful deep-sea diver, or there can be less emphasis on application and more on abstract outcomes such as knowledge of history or politics. This does not mean that transfer is not still a consideration; it simply indicates that it can be assessed in a less formal way that can be decided by the educator and participants rather than by external stakeholders.

The evaluation system in different teaching contexts can reflect a greater or lesser interest in transfer of learning. This can range from student evaluation sheets, with a question like "Do you think what you have learned in this course will be useful at work?" to elaborate follow-ups involving surveys completed by participants six months after the course. It is becoming more expected that agencies receiving funding for education will produce long-term data about the effectiveness of their programs, which very often comes down to the degree to which new knowledge proved to be applicable.

It is not surprising that the context of application makes a very significant difference to transfer of learning, and there are two especially important factors. The first is the degree of support for application, which varies enormously. Some writers recommend working with supervisors in designing staff development to ensure they buy into the process and its outcomes and will support implementation of the new knowledge (Taylor, 1997). This can be a complicated and expensive business in some cases, as access to managers can be limited. When the context for application is not a workplace, it can be impossible to involve everybody potentially affected by the transfer of learning. In some cases it may be more effective and helpful to support the learners' commitment to applying new knowledge rather than try to change the context.

The second consideration is the feasibility of application. It may simply be too difficult or expensive to transfer the new way that an individual has learned to do something into a new context. If seniors learn to use social media to keep in touch with their grandchildren in a community center class, transfer to their home lives means that they need a computer and connectivity in the home. Some will be able to afford this and some will not; even though the latter group has learned as much as the former group, transfer will be much more challenging.

Whatever the context, the degree of thought given to the possibility of application by educator and learners will make a huge difference to the ease of transfer. The teaching and learning environment can go a long way toward making transfer desirable and effective for all involved.

Allyson can see the potential context for application of the team approach very clearly, and she understands the sticking points. Primarily they have to do with a lot of busy people who are used to doing things in a specific way and who may feel they don't have the time to reinvent the wheel for advantages that appear a bit nebulous. The real powerbrokers may not be interested in team approaches. However, Allyson realizes that transfer could be far more effective if it were less "all or nothing." With this in mind, she starts to think about asking program participants to build mini-teams among themselves and a small number of like-minded staff such as technologists. If this is successful, it's likely the approach will spread and broader implementation will be easier. Allyson realizes that rather than refusing to change her approach to teaching and getting nowhere, she can allow the transfer challenges to shape her teaching in positive and valuable ways.

CONCLUSION

The main point of this chapter has been to emphasize the importance of designing courses to support transfer of learning. With good strategies in place, learners can come out of programs with new ways of seeing the world and possibilities for acting on those new perspectives. On the one hand, considerations of transfer are deeply pragmatic, but on the other, I think that they can be seen as an important philosophical commitment by educators to making their courses as valuable as possible for learners. Whether we are teaching the most abstract or the most concrete subjects, it can be beneficial to think through the utility and application of what we teach. With this in mind, I now return to the questions raised at the beginning of the chapter.

What sort of transfer is possible?

Understanding the possibilities for transfer is important for educators and for learners. There are concrete barriers to transfer, such as resources, and cultural ones, such as established practices. The role of the educator is to work with the learners to ensure that the best possible transfer occurs.

What is the boundary for transfer?

This question asks us to think about what we are hoping learners will transfer, and where they will transfer it to. This information will help with the design of the program and the strategies for transfer, as well as make it much easier to determine whether transfer is taking place. For example, if I am working with a group of community members on transportation issues for disabled citizens, the boundary for transfer may not be clear. Is it between the group who are working together to develop strategies and the actions they take to support the issue elsewhere, or is it between this specific issue and the participants' general level of political involvement? Both are realistic and valuable forms of transfer, but knowing which is my aim will help me to understand how to support transfer and what it might look like.

How can transfer of learning be demonstrated?

In some contexts there are complex mechanisms to monitor the transfer that is taking place; in others there are none at all. Even if there are no explicit expectations, it can be very useful for educators to have a sense of the degree to which what they are teaching has an ongoing impact. If nothing else, informally following up with students after courses have ended can provide fascinating and useful insights.

What are the viable strategies to support transfer?

This is where the educator can draw on the expertise of the learners to understand what is more likely to help with application. Using the insider knowledge of the learners to ensure that the possibilities and challenges are known by all involved can make courses more useful and also increase their credibility.

What are the expectations of transfer?

In some settings the expectations are high; in others they are never discussed. Teaching will be influenced by these expectations, so it can be important to know about them. Discussions with colleagues in the educational setting and with learners are very valuable here.

What opportunities does the educator have to influence transfer?

The key opportunities for the educator are in building strategies for transfer into the course design, which requires some knowledge of the context of application. The role of the educator is to support the participants to develop their own knowledge of how application can and should be taking place. In the end, it is the learners who will transfer the knowledge if it is credible and feasible.

As with a number of the other design elements discussed in this book, transfer of learning could well be taken as the central dimension of teaching adults, with the other elements supporting it. This really shows how much these elements need to be brought together in an effective course, and also how much potential there is in transfer of learning to help us think about the teaching we do.

chapter TEN

Design Frames Practice

Throughout this book I have used the idea of design as a way to emphasize that education for adults comes about like every other human endeavor—through a series of deliberate and informed decisions. The aim of this book was not to provide a list of ways to do things but to highlight the sorts of questions that a responsible and reflective educator needs to think about in making the necessary decisions. I believe that each educator must develop a style of teaching that reflects her own interests and philosophy, and that there is no way that any author can shortcut that process. Over time, as educators gain experience, they can become better at addressing the questions so that it goes more quickly for each course, but this reflects a long-term commitment to development as an educator. In other words, it can be learned, but not easily taught. Nevertheless, there are some starting points that may be helpful to educators as they begin to take on that commitment. In this chapter I pull together the discussion of those starting points, presented in the rest of the book, into a framework for designing education for adults.

THE BOOK IN A BOX

I am a big fan of visual learning, so I wanted to provide a diagram that could summarize everything we have talked about in this book at a glance. Figure 10.1 presents that diagram, with the key ideas and questions from the opening of chapters Four through Nine. The diagram is *not* in the form of a list, which can sometimes suggest, however subconsciously, that things have to happen in a certain order. Instead, the six design elements discussed in depth are arranged around the three central influences common to them all: the educator (or educators), the learners, and the context. Because the diagram manages to pack almost two hundred pages of discussion into a single graphic, I have come to think of it as the "book in a box."

I am not going to run through all of the questions that appear in the diagram—after all, the whole point of a diagram is to convey that type of information. I do have a few general comments.

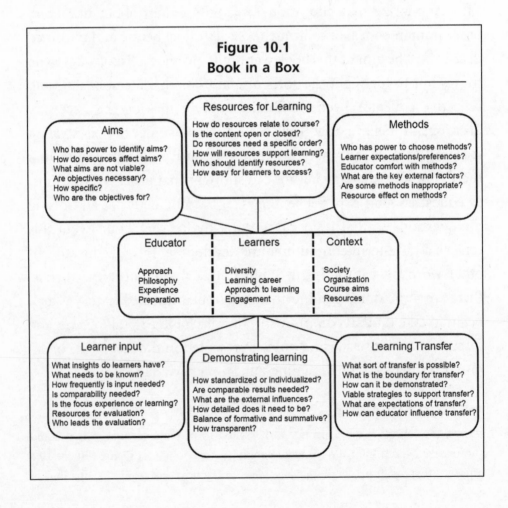

Figure 10.1
Book in a Box

Resources for Learning
How do resources relate to course?
Is the content open or closed?
Do resources need a specific order?
How will resources support learning?
Who should identify resources?
How easy for learners to access?

Aims
Who has power to identify aims?
How do resources affect aims?
What aims are not viable?
Are objectives necessary?
How specific?
Who are the objectives for?

Methods
Who has power to choose methods?
Learner expectations/preferences?
Educator comfort with methods?
What are the key external factors?
Are some methods inappropriate?
Resource effect on methods?

Educator
Approach
Philosophy
Experience
Preparation

Learners
Diversity
Learning career
Approach to learning
Engagement

Context
Society
Organization
Course aims
Resources

Learner input
What insights do learners have?
What needs to be known?
How frequently is input needed?
Is comparability needed?
Is the focus experience or learning?
Resources for evaluation?
Who leads the evaluation?

Demonstrating learning
How standardized or individualized?
Are comparable results needed?
What are the external influences?
How detailed does it need to be?
Balance of formative and summative?
How transparent?

Learning Transfer
What sort of transfer is possible?
What is the boundary for transfer?
How can it be demonstrated?
Viable strategies to support transfer?
What are expectations of transfer?
How can educator influence transfer?

I believe very strongly that educators need to recognize the importance of the three central factors. To some extent, everything that surrounds them flows out of those elements. If you know yourself as an educator, have a good grasp on the learning careers and expectations of learners, and have a degree of insight into the nature and power structures of your teaching context, then the choices open to you are generally quite clear. If you understand these three critical starting points, it is much easier to build the program out from them.

When looking at the diagram, with its six design elements ranged around the central elements, it can be helpful to bear in mind that the elements are strongly linked, and not always in the most intuitive way. For example, aims and methods tend to be aligned, which does not seem very surprising. Where the course is going and how it will get there would tend to influence each other. However, evaluation—meaning the way that learners provide input on the course—is more strongly aligned with transfer than it is with assessment of learning. As I suggested in Chapter Nine, this is because a course that is seen as credible by learners, and therefore evaluated positively, is more likely to give participants learning that they want to transfer. Assessment can be seen as more of an abstract measurement of learning than a real predictor of the application of new knowledge, and it seems to be connected only loosely to course evaluations. So learner satisfaction may not predict learning very well (at least on a measurable level) but may increase the likelihood that whatever learning does take place will be applied.

On scanning the design elements, you should, I believe, see a level of consistency. So if you see yourself as a radical, change-the-world sort of educator but you are giving lectures and exams, you may want to think about why this is the case. I'm certainly not saying that such combinations are impossible or necessarily ineffective, but educators may want to give them some thought when they see them, and consider why that potential inconsistency is there.

I believe that learning experiences can appear seamless to learners, and the more aligned the design elements are, the more seamless they will appear. This may or may not be a good thing, depending on your context. If you are hoping that people will come out of your course with knowledge about the concrete processes of knowledge creation and exchange, such as a "train the trainer" program, a little less seamlessness can be good. I recently taught a course on teaching adults in which I deliberately tried to let the cracks and difficulties of that course show so participants would get a real-life case study and experience of how courses are actually put together.

However well the course is designed and however much preparatory time the educator devotes to the class, there will always be participants who are more or less fond of a course. You can never make a design that addresses everybody's needs and preferences equally. In suggesting that courses should be designed, I am not saying they can be made risk free. During the course I mentioned in the preceding paragraph, some people saw what I was trying to do and said it was the best course ever, because they had an opportunity to see a course being constructed. But others hated it, because they wanted a far more linear delivery of "things to do when you teach." Neither group is more right, but it would have been very difficult to design a course they both would have liked. Nonetheless, the program design framework can help educators to recognize some of the competing values and respond to them.

AN EXAMPLE OF A PROGRAM DESIGN

To make the diagram—and, I hope, the framework generally—more concrete, Figure 10.2 shows what it might look like once completed. For this example I have adopted the perspective of a trades instructor in a college. In the middle I jotted down a couple of notes about the values I would bring to teaching, who the learners are, and the aims of the course. You don't always need to write a great deal here; it is really meant to focus graphically on the key points. Then I moved on to complete the six design elements.

In filling in the design elements, I did not start at one end and work my way round. I did begin with aims, but that led me to move to demonstration of learning and learning transfer, before coming back to the in-class elements and then back to other parts again. Ideas about one element inevitably spark ways of thinking about others.

If this chart is compared with the original, it is clear that I did not answer all the questions, because some of them were less relevant. I also combined a few answers, such as "Educator likes practical work, and resources are available" (in Methods), which covers teaching style and one of the resource questions. It also made sense to include a few "notes to myself" here as I went along, such as "Include online videos learners can watch at home" and "Learners can add specific objectives

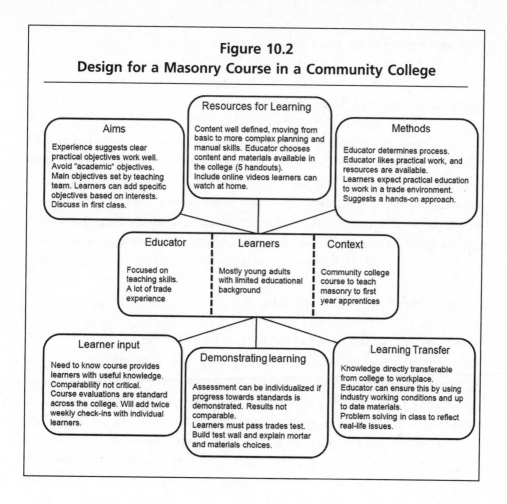

Figure 10.2
Design for a Masonry Course in a Community College

Resources for Learning
Content well defined, moving from basic to more complex planning and manual skills. Educator chooses content and materials available in the college (5 handouts). Include online videos learners can watch at home.

Aims
Experience suggests clear practical objectives work well. Avoid "academic" objectives. Main objectives set by teaching team. Learners can add specific objectives based on interests. Discuss in first class.

Methods
Educator determines process. Educator likes practical work, and resources are available. Learners expect practical education to work in a trade environment. Suggests a hands-on approach.

Educator
Focused on teaching skills. A lot of trade experience

Learners
Mostly young adults with limited educational background

Context
Community college course to teach masonry to first year apprentices

Learner input
Need to know course provides learners with useful knowledge. Comparability not critical. Course evaluations are standard across the college. Will add twice weekly check-ins with individual learners.

Demonstrating learning
Assessment can be individualized if progress towards standards is demonstrated. Results not comparable. Learners must pass trades test. Build test wall and explain mortar and materials choices.

Learning Transfer
Knowledge directly transferable from college to workplace. Educator can ensure this by using industry working conditions and up to date materials. Problem solving in class to reflect real-life issues.

based on their experience. Discuss in first class." The point of the diagram is to bridge between the big questions of design, which can often be abstract and almost theoretical, and the real-life questions about the practices I would use in the class to teach this subject.

FOR NEW EDUCATORS OF ADULTS

It's Thursday at 4.30 P.M., almost time to go home. Your boss walks into your office at the insurance company (you manage to look busy!) and says, "You know your way around our records system. I would like you to provide a two-hour session to our eleven new clerks on Monday at ten. Okay?"

After the initial moment of confusion, you realize that you have no choice; you smile shakily and say "Of course, no problem." You had meant to spend the weekend camping, but instead you are at home in front of a computer as you try to pull something together. You end up with a presentation with 107 slides (but some nifty animations) and wonder *Is there a better way to do this?*

This is how many people begin their careers as educators of adults. For most of us, it's not something we plan for or are trained for, but rather something that happens, as John Lennon said about life, "while you're busy making other plans."

In this section I lay out some actions for first-time educators who need to pull something together really quickly. What I have done is distill the design framework into one question for each element. If you can answer each of these questions, it will not completely design the course, but it will give you a good starting point, whether for your two-hour session with new clerks, a semester-long course on masonry, or a drop-in program on literacy and second language. There are nine questions.

The Educator: What's Important to You in a Teacher?

You can learn a lot about your own teaching style from the way you like to be taught. If you like a teacher with a sense of humor, chances are you will use humor in your own teaching. If you have only a short time to pull a course together, it makes sense to use the strengths you already possess. Thinking about teachers you've liked will also give you clues to the sorts of things that are important to you, such as critical thinking or precise details. This can help you decide what to emphasize more or less in your teaching, given the people who will be in the class.

The Learners: What Will Ensure They Are Engaged in the Course?

The key challenge in working with learners, from which everything else flows, is keeping them engaged. If learners are engaged, they will be motivated and interested; if not, you may as well go home. In this book I've discussed a number of the factors that affect learner engagement from a more abstract perspective. If you have a course to teach on Monday, keep one thing in mind: the quickest way to lose engagement is to follow your agenda and not the interests of the learners. This happens all the time, and it's very seductive for educators. So start planning around "What are learners likely to be interested in?" and then "What ways of teaching this would be interesting?" and you will not go too far wrong. (Tip: 107 slides is probably too many!)

The Context: How Can the Context Help You to Teach?

There are lots of questions that can be asked about the context, and they are important. But if you have time for only one question, this has to be it. It focuses on the positive effects, which are what you need to know, and in answering it, some of the limits of the context will become apparent. The key point is that any context has elements that make your job easier, and it's good to start from those. It's worth noting that these may not always be things you agree with. For example, you may not like the fact that you will be teaching to a test of some sort, but on one level, it does clarify your job as an educator.

Aims: What Are People There to Learn?

This appears to be a really simple question, but of course it isn't. The first thing to notice is that I haven't asked "What are you there to teach?" Knowing what people are there to learn necessarily involves talking to learners to find out. Generally, I find that there is a set of formal aims of the course, a set of things learners are interested in, and ideally an area of overlap that is the "sweet spot" for the educator to work in. Learners can often deal with some content that is not within their interests, but if the whole course does not match what they hope for, this is a problem.

Resources for Learning: What Has the Highest Priority?

In thinking about content, start with the time you have. Work out what you can cover in that time, then take out half of it. Then organize what is left in terms of priority. Educators almost always try to cover too much material and content, and this is especially true for new educators, who may gain some comfort from having three binders full of content for a thirty-minute session (at least they won't run out of things to say!). I have to admit I still do the same thing after thirty years; there is virtue in "cutting to the chase" and dealing with the most important area first so that they aren't packed into the last ten minutes.

Methods: What Sort of Relationship with the Learners Will Support Engagement?

When thinking about teaching methods that support engagement, you are actually thinking about the forms of relationship that you can help to build in the course. To a great extent this has to be driven by the learners—their expectations and their preferences. A misjudgment about process pretty much undermines engagement, whether the educator is too formal for a community setting or too relaxed for the workplace. When you have a good idea of what the relationship should look like, it is relatively straightforward to think about ways of teaching that fit with this relationship. For example, if the relationship should be one of expert and students, then the methods should be less collective than if the relationship was one of colleagues working on a problem together. Generally, the more collective and participatory the methods, the more effective and engaging they will be.

Learner Input: How Can You Find Out If the Class Is Working for Learners?

As an educator, your job is to support learning. To find out whether you are doing that, you need to ask learners and find out how they are getting on. To do this safely, you often need to offer anonymity, which in most cases means written feedback (either in paper or online). This does not have to be a complicated process, but it does need to be thought about and planned in advance.

Demonstrating Learning: How Can Learning Become Visible?

You do want to have a sense that learners are meeting the aims of the course, even if there is no formal assessment tool. The easiest question to ask to get you thinking about this area is how learners can show what they've learned. This can range from the most practical task to an elaborate series of demonstrations. Generally, I advise educators to be imaginative and have fun with this aspect of the work. One very useful technique is asking learners to do something and then asking them why they decided to do it that way. The educator can learn very quickly how learners are thinking about the task and how informed it is by the content of the course.

Learning Transfer: How Can You Bring Learning as Close as Possible to the Application?

For cutting through the complexities of making sure that what people learn is useful for them, this question is an effective starting point. If the course can be built around modeling the ways knowledge can be applied, it can strengthen the potential for application substantially. At the simplest level, this could involve our fictional insurance trainer working through lots of examples and setting up scenarios for the learners to discuss among themselves. Over time, educators who teach the same topic often find increasingly sophisticated and effective ways to bring learning and application closer together.

CONCLUSION

In this brief chapter I have pulled together the strands of the previous discussions and provided some very pragmatic entry points into a complex vocation. Teaching adults is not easy; challenges and failures come with the territory, however long you have been doing it. But it is also some of the most rewarding work that I can think of. When it is going well, both the learners and the educators get a feeling that I think of as being like travelling in a sailboat when the wind and the heading are just right. There is an incredibly powerful feeling that something bigger than the boat is in charge and that you just have to ride along.

Just like sailing the sailboat, this does not happen by accident in teaching adults. It happens because a lot of thought, time, and talent have gone into design. In this book I have tried to lay out the most important aspects of design, but as educators gain experience, their knowledge of the decisions that have to be made and the answers that will work for them will expand and deepen. I wish you success—and fun—on that voyage.

REFERENCES

Anderson, T., & Elloumi, F. (2004). *Theory and practice of online learning*. Athabasca, AB: Athabasca University.

Auerbach, S. (2007). From moral supporters to struggling advocates: Reconceptualizing parent roles in education through the experience of working-class families of color. *Urban Education, 43*(3), 250–283.

Bandura, A. (2004). Health promotion by social cognitive means. *Health Education & Behavior, 31*(2), 143–164.

Beer, C. T., & Darkenwald, G. G. (1989). Gender differences in adult student perceptions of college classroom social environments. *Adult Education Quarterly 40*(1), 33–42.

Belenky, M. F., Clinchy, B. M., Goldberger, N. R., & Tarule, J. M. (1997). *Women's ways of knowing: The development of self, voice, and mind*. New York: Basic Books.

Boshier, R. B. (2000). Theoretical perspectives on learning for prevention of fishing vessel accidents. *Canadian Journal for the Study of Adult Learning 14*(2), 49–66.

Brookfield, S. D. (1995). *Becoming a critically reflective teacher*. San Francisco: Jossey-Bass.

Brookfield, S. D., with Preskill, S. (2005). *Discussion as a way of teaching*. San Francisco: Jossey-Bass.

Burgstahler, S. (2012). Universal design of instruction: Definition, principles, guidelines and examples. Retrieved from http://www.washington.edu/doit/Brochures/PDF/instruction.pdf

Caffarella, R. S. (2002). *Planning programs for adult learners: A practical guide for educators, trainers, and staff developers*. New York: Jossey-Bass.

Cervero, R. M., & Wilson, A. L. (1994). *Planning responsibly for adult education: A guide to negotiating power and interests*. San Francisco: Jossey-Bass.

Clayson, D. E. (2009). Student evaluations of teaching: Are they related to what students learn? A meta-analysis and review of the literature. *Journal of Marketing Education, 31*, 16–30.

Closson, R. B. (2010). Critical race theory and adult education. *Adult Education Quarterly, 60*(3), 261–283.

Crossan, B., Field, J., Gallacher, J., & Merrill, B. (2003). Understanding participation in learning for non-traditional adult learners: Learning careers and the construction of learning identities. *British Journal of Sociology of Education, 24*(1), 55–67.

Daffron, S. R., & North, M. W. (2011). *Successful transfer of learning.* Malaber, FL: Krieger.

Edson, J. (2013). *Design like Apple: Seven principles for creating insanely great products, services, and experiences.* New York: Wiley.

Elias, J. T., & Merriam, S. B. (1995). *Philosophical Foundations of Adult Education.* Malabar, FL: Kreiger.

European Commission. (2001). *Communiqué: Making a European area of lifelong learning a reality.* Brussels: European Commission.

Evans, R. I. (1989). *Albert Bandura: The man and his ideas.* New York: Praeger.

Fenwick, T., & Parsons, J. (2000). *The art of evaluation: A handbook for educators and trainers.* Toronto: Thompson Educational.

Field, J. (2009). Learning transitions in the adult life course: Agency, identity and social capital. In B. Merrill (Ed.), *Learning to change? The role of identity and learning careers in adult education* (pp. 17–31). Frankfurt-am-Main, Germany: Peter Lang.

Findsen, B., & Formosa, M. (2011). *Lifelong learning in later life: A handbook on older adult learning.* Rotterdam: Sense.

Foster, M. (1994). The power to know one thing is never the power to know all things: Methodological notes on two studies of Black American teachers. In A. Griffin (Ed.), *Power and method: Political activism and educational research* (pp. 129–146). New York: Routledge.

Freire, P. (1971). *Pedagogy of the oppressed.* Harmondsworth, UK: Penguin.

Gilligan, C. (1982). *In a different voice: Psychological theory and women's development.* Cambridge, MA: Harvard University Press.

Grace, A., & Wells, K. (2007). Using Freirean pedagogy of just ire to inform critical social learning in arts-informed community education for sexual minorities. *Adult Education Quarterly, 57*(2), 95–114.

Gunn, V. (2010). *Lesbian, gay, bisexual, and transgender (LGBT) perspectives and learning at university.* Glasgow: University of Glasgow Teaching and Learning Services.

Haggis, T. (2002). Exploring the "black box" of process: A comparison of theoretical notions of the "adult learner" with accounts of postgraduate learning experience. *Studies in Higher Education, 27*(2), 207–220.

Hansman, C. A. (2001). Context-based adult learning. In S. Merriam (Ed.), *The new update on adult learning theory.* New Directions for Adult and Continuing Education, no. 89. San Francisco: Wiley.

Hayes, E. (1989). New insights from women's experience for teaching and learning. In E. Hayes (Ed.), *Effective teaching styles.* New Directions for Continuing Education, no. 43 (pp. 55–66). San Francisco: Jossey-Bass.

Houle, C. O. (1972). *The design of education.* San Francisco: Jossey-Bass.

Hughes, S. A., & Berry, T. R. (2012). *The evolving significance of race: Living, learning, and teaching*. New York: Peter Lang.

Hunn, L. M. (2004). Africentric philosophy: A remedy for Eurocentric dominance. In R. St. Clair & J. A. Sandlin (Eds.), New Directions for Adult and Continuing Education, no. 102 (pp. 65–74). San Francisco: Wiley.

Jarvis-Selinger, S., Collins, J. B., & Pratt, D. D. (2007). Do academic origins influence perspectives on teaching? *Teacher Education Quarterly, 33*(3), 67–81.

Jones, P. (2010). Equality and Human Rights Commission Triennial Review: Education (Lifelong Learning). Participation in Adult Learning. Southampton, UK: University of Southampton.

Joseph Rowntree Foundation. (2007). *Experiences of poverty and educational disadvantage.* York, UK: Joseph Rowntree Foundation.

Kaminsky, J. A., Sloutsky, V. M., & Heckler, A. F. (2005, July). *Relevant concreteness and its effects on learning and transfer.* Paper presented at the annual conference of the Cognitive Science Society, Stresa, Italy.

Kelly, T. (1992). *A history of adult education in Great Britain from the middle ages to the twentieth century.* Liverpool, UK: Liverpool University Press.

King, D. (2012). New perspectives on context-based chemistry education: Using a dialectical sociocultural approach to view teaching and learning. *Studies in Science Education, 48*(1), 51–87.

Knowles, M. S. (1980). *The modern practice of adult education.* Englewood Cliffs, NJ: Prentice Hall.

Knowles, M. S., Holton, E. F., & Swanson, R. A. (1998). *The adult learner: The definitive classic in adult education and human resource development.* Houston, TX: Gulf Publishing.

Kolb, D. (1984). *Experiential learning: Experience as the source of learning and development.* Englewood Cliffs, NJ: Prentice Hall.

Kraiger, K., Ford, J. K., & Salas, E. (1993). Application of cognitive, skills-based, and affective theories of learning outcomes to new methods of training evaluation. *Journal of Applied Psychology, 78*(2), 311–328.

Larsson, S., & Norvall, H. (2010). *Study circles in Sweden: An overview with a bibliography of international literature.* Linköping, Sweden: Linköping University Electronic Press.

Lave, J., & Wegner, E. (1991). *Situated learning: Legitimate peripheral participation.* New York: Cambridge University Press.

Leicester, M. (2001). Two decades of feminist theory—and beyond. *International Journal of Lifelong Education, 20*(1/2), 55–62.

Lund, C. L. (2010). The nature of White privilege in the teaching and training of adults. In C. L. Lund & S.A.J. Colin, III (Eds.), New Directions for Adult and Continuing Education, no. 125 (pp. 15–25). San Francisco: Wiley.

Mason, G. (2010). *Adult learning in decline? Recent evidence at UK national and city-region level.* Centre for Learning and Life Chances in Knowledge Economies and Societies. Retrieved from http://www.llakes.org

McGivney, V. (1999). *Returning women: Their training and employment choices and needs.* Leicester, UK: NIACE.

McTighe, J., & Brown, J. L. (2005). Differentiated instruction and educational standards: Is detente possible? *Theory into Practice, 44*(3), 234–244.

Merriam, S. B., & Caffarella, R. S. (1999). *Learning in adulthood: A comprehensive guide.* San Francisco: Jossey-Bass.

Merriam, S. B., & Leahy, B. (2005). Learning transfer: A review of the research in adult education and training. *PAACE Journal of Lifelong Learning, 14*(1), 1–24.

Mezirow, J. (1995). Transformation theory of adult learning. In M. R. Welton (Ed.), *In defense of the lifeworld* (pp. 39–70). Albany, NY: State University of New York.

Murnane, R. J., & Phillips, B. R. (1981). Learning by doing, vintage, and selection: Three pieces of the puzzle relating teaching experience and teaching performance. *Economics of Education Review, 1*(4), 453–465.

National Association of Pharmacy Regulatory Authorities/Association nationale des organismes de réglementation de la pharmacie (2007). *Professional competencies for Canadian pharmacists at entry to practice.* Ottawa: National Association of Pharmacy Regulatory Authorities.

Nesbit, T. (2006). What's the matter with social class? *Adult Education Quarterly, 56*(3), 171–187.

Ottoson, J. M. (1997). After the applause: Exploring multiple influences on application following an adult education program. *Adult Education Quarterly, 47*(2), 92–107.

Perry, W. G. (1970). *Forms of intellectual and ethical development in the college years: A scheme.* New York: Holt, Rinehart, and Winston.

Pirsig, R. M. (1974). *Zen and the art of motorcycle maintenance: An inquiry into values.* New York: Morrow.

Pratt, D. D. (1992). Conceptions of teaching. *Adult Education Quarterly, 42*(4), 203–220.

Pratt, D. D. (2002). Good teaching: One size fits all? In J. Ross-Gordon (Ed), *Special Issue: Contemporary Viewpoints on Teaching Adults Effectively* (pp. 5–15). New Directions in Adult and Continuing Education, no. 93. San Francisco: Wiley.

Rabinowitz, W., & Rosenbaum, I. (1960). Teacher experience and teachers' attitudes. *The Elementary School Journal, 60*(6), 313–319.

Rocco, T., & West, G. W. (1998). Deconstructing privilege: An examination of privilege in adult education. *Adult Education Quarterly, 48*(3), 171–184.

Rogers, A. (1986). *Teaching adults.* Milton Keynes, UK: Open University Press.

Sabates, R., Feinstein, L., & Skaliotis, E. (2007). *Determinants and pathways of progression to level 2 qualifications: Evidence from the NCDS and BHPS.* London: Centre for Research on the Wider Benefits of Learning.

San Francisco Museum of Modern Art. (2011). *SFMOMA presents less and more: The design ethos of Dieter Rams*. Retrieved from http://www.sfmoma.org/about/press/press_exhibitions/releases/880

Santamaria, L. J. (2009). Culturally responsive differentiated instruction: Narrowing gaps between best pedagogical practices benefiting all learners. *Teachers College Record*, *111*(1), 214–227.

Sargant, N., & Aldridge, F. (2002). *Adult learning and social division: A persistent pattern*. Leicester, UK: NIACE.

Schön, D. A. (1983). *The reflective practitioner: How professionals think in action*. New York: Basic Books.

Seaman, D. F., & Fellenz, D. F. (1989). *Effective strategies for teaching adults*. Columbus, OH: Merrill.

Simon, H. A. (1981). *The sciences of the artificial*. Cambridge, MA: MIT Press.

Siragusa, L., Dixon, K. C., & Dixon, R. (2007, December). *Designing quality e-learning environments in higher education*. Paper presented at the Australian Society for Computers in Learning in Tertiary Education conference, Singapore.

Skinner, B. F. (1965). *Science and human behavior*. New York: Free Press.

Smith, B. J., & Delahaye, B. L. (1987). *How to be an effective trainer* (2nd ed.). New York: Wiley.

Smith, C., Hofer, J., Gillespie, M., Solomon, M., & Rowe, K. (2003). *How teachers change: A study of professional development in adult education. NCSALL Report #25*. Cambridge, MA: National Center for the Study of Adult Literacy and Learning.

Solorzano, D., Ceja, M., & Yosso, T. (2000). Critical race theory, racial microaggressions, and campus racial climate: The experiences of African American college students. *Journal of Negro Education*, *69*(1/2), 60–73.

Sork, T. J. (2000). Planning educational programs. In A. L. Wilson & E. R. Hayes (Eds.), *Handbook of adult and continuing education* (pp. 171–190). San Francisco: Jossey-Bass.

Sork, T. J. (2010). Planning and delivering programs. In C. E. Kasworm, A. D. Rose, & J. M. Ross-Gordon (Eds.), *Handbook of adult and continuing education* (pp. 157–166). Washington, DC: Sage/AAACE.

Spooren, P., Brockx, B., & Mortelmans, D. (2013). On the validity of student evaluation of teaching: The state of the art. *Review of Educational Research* (currently in Online First).

Stromquist, N. (2013). Adult education of women for social transformation: Reviving the promise, continuing the struggle. In T. Nesbit & M. Welton (Eds.), New Directions in Adult and Continuing Education, no. 138 (pp. 29–38). San Francisco: Wiley.

Tamburri, R. (2013). *Trend to measure learning outcomes gain proponents*. University Affairs, February 6. Retrieved from http://www.universityaffairs.ca/trend-to-measure-learning-outcomes-gains-proponents.aspx

Taylor, E. (2003). The relationship between the prior school lives of adult educators and their beliefs about teaching adults. *International Journal of Lifelong Education, 22*(1), 59–77.

Taylor, M. (1997). *Transfer of learning: Planning effective workplace education programs.* Ottawa: HRSDC, National Literacy Secretariat.

Tisdell, E. J. (1998). Poststructural feminist pedagogies: The possibilities and limitations of feminist emancipatory adult learning theory and practice. *Adult Education Quarterly, 48*(3), 139–156.

Tomlinson, C. A. (1999). *The differentiated classroom: Responding to the needs of all learners.* Alexandria, VA: Association for Supervision and Curriculum Development.

Tuckett, A., & Aldridge, F. (2008). Are we closing the gap? A NIACE briefing on participation in learning by adults from minority ethnic groups. Leicester, UK: National Institute of Adult Continuing Education.

Tyler, R. W. (1949). *Basic principles of curriculum and instruction.* Chicago: University of Chicago.

Van Eekelen, I. M., Boshuizen, H.P.A., & Vermunt, J. D. (2005). Self-regulation in higher education teacher learning. *Higher Education, 50,* 447–471.

Vygotsky, L. S. (1978). *Mind in society* (M. Cole, V. John-Steiner, S. Scribner, & E. Souberman, Eds.) Cambridge, MA: Harvard University Press.

Waldron, M. W., & Moore, G. A. S. (1991). *Helping adults learn.* Toronto: Thomson.

Watson, J. B. (1913). Psychology as the behaviorist views it. *Psychological Review, 20,* 158–177.

Zinn, L. M. (1983). Development of a valid and reliable instrument to identify a personal philosophy of adult education. Florida State University: unpublished doctoral dissertation. *Dissertation Abstracts International, 44,* 1667A.

A Blank Design Framework

When it comes time to design your own course, it may be helpful to work through the areas and questions as we have done in this book. I hope this blank design framework, to be copied or cut out and kept, will be useful to you in this process.

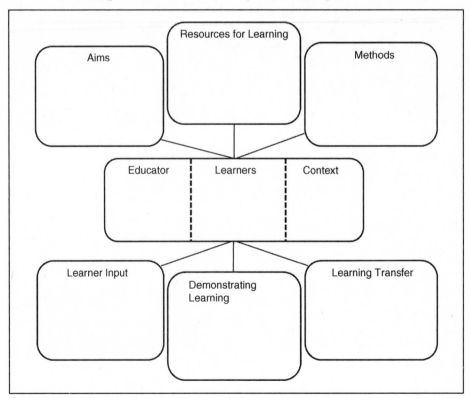

Where to Find Further Resources

As mentioned earlier, there seems little point in providing an exhaustive and detailed list of resources when the online world is changing so fast! However, there are a number of organizations doing a terrific job of indexing the changing resources. The following list includes only resources that have been stable for a number of years and that consistently provide high-quality information that will be useful to readers of this book. You'll be surprised how good some of these resources are. Have fun exploring.

ERIC database from the Institute of Education Sciences, Washington, DC (www.eric.ed.gov)

This service has been around since 1964 and remains one of the key resources for educators. It contains a listing of thousands of journals, conference papers, and books on education generally and many on education for adults. A quick search for "group work" turns up thirty-eight thousand hits. The results may give you information and a link, an abstract, or a full paper. A lot of the resources are practical rather than academic. Strongly recommended.

Northwest Center for Public Health Practice, University of Washington (www.nwcphp.org/documents/training/tools-resources)

This center has done a good job of published training for educators, and it is well worth checking out what they have to offer. The resources tend to be very well written and clear. There's a lot of health-oriented information, but a good general selection as well.

INFED, YMCA George Williams College (www.infed.org)

One of my favorite resources, this is a superb source for information on adult learning, particularly informal approaches. Go here to learn about community-based initiatives, Paulo Freire, and lots more!

Literacy Information and Communication System (www.lincs.ed.gov)

This U.S. government system provides information and training for adult educators, with a particular emphasis on literacy. There are free downloadable PDF books on a range of topics as well as online education for educators.

Office of Career, Technical, and Adult Education, U.S. Government (www2.ed .gov/about/offices/list/ovae/index.html)

Another U.S. government site with a wealth of information. In this case, the community college and vocational aspects are best represented, with a range of free resources for community college teaching in particular. There is good representation of material on the experiences of different ethnic groups in the United States, for example.

National Research and Development Centre for Adult Literacy and Numeracy (www.nrdc.org.uk/index.asp)

This British organization is dedicated to developing practice and knowledge in literacy, numeracy, English as a second language, and adult learning more generally. There is a good section of practitioner resources, some freely available and some with a low cost.

YouTube (www.youtube.com)

It may seem a bit ridiculous to include such a general resource, but there is a surprisingly wide and useful selection of videos on YouTube related to education for adults, ranging from "how to teach" to subject-specific resources.

Teacher Excellence in Adult Literacy Center (www.teal.ed.gov)

This site for a multistate initiative features a number of great resources that go far beyond literacy. In particular, they have published an excellent resource on universal design, available as a free PDF at https://teal.ed.gov/documents/ TEAL_JustWriteGuide.pdf

INDEX

Page numbers followed by *f* and *t* refer to figures and tables, respectively.

Google hangouts, 116
Grades, 155
Group presentations, 154
Guest speakers, 119

H
Haggis, T., 34
Hands-on activities, 124
Hansman, C. A., 54
Harvard University, 19
Hayes, E., 41
Honesty, xvii
Houle, C. O., 98
Humanist view, of education, 12

I
Identity:
   of educators, 16–18
   sexual, 45
Individuals, teaching methods with,
      115t, 116–117
Individualized assessments, 152–153,
   165
Individualized objectives, 83
INFED, 202
Informal learning, 56–58, 178–179
Information:
   from assessments, 150–152
   content as, 98–99
   from evaluations, 139
   preferences for receiving, 46
   sharing, in online courses,
      60–61
   transmission of, in teaching, 6
Innovation, xvi

Intentions:
   of educators, 4
   of learners, 32
Interaction, professional development
      through, 19–20
iPad, xv–xvi
Isomorphism, 172–173

J
Journals, 116–117, 154

K
Knowles, M. S., 31–32
Kolb, D., 173

L
Large groups, teaching methods with,
      115t, 119–120
Learners, xiii, 23–52
   and assessments, 154, 159–162
   diversity of, 36–52
   emotional comfort of, 124
   engagement of, 30–36
   and learner input, 140–142
   and learning process, 24–30
   and methods, 123–125, 128
   motivation of, 23
   perceptions of learning by, 142
   and resources for learning,
      105–106
   tasks of, 114–115, 115t
   time investment of, 67–68
   and transfer of learning, 171–172,
      176–178
Learner-centeredness, 121–122

National Center for the Study of Adult Literacy and Learning, 19
National Research and Development Centre for Adult Literacy and Numeracy, 202
"Need to know," 171–172
Negotiation:
    of objectives, 86
    and power, xv
    as role of educators, 64
Nesbit, T., 44
New educators, tips for, 187–191
Non-contact time, contact vs., 67
Non-formal learning, 56–58
North, M. W., 169
Northwest Center for Public Health Practice, 201–202
Nurturing perspective, 14

O
Objectives, 77–94
    and assessment, 83–84
    and available resources, 92–93
    and behaviorism, 80–81
    and competencies, 83
    and content, 109
    and context, 90–92
    educators and, 86–87
    in formal learning, 81
    intention of, 93
    learners and, 88–89, 189
    and learning, 88–89
    not using, 85
    overly defined or vague, 84–85
    power to define, 92

precision of, 81
resources on, 81
reviewing, 82
specific vs. general, 83, 93
standardization of, 90–91
unachievable, 93
uniform vs. individualized, 83
value of having, 80, 84, 93–94
Office of Vocational and Adult Education, 202
Online education:
    accessibility of, 106
    context with, 59–62
    and methods, 116, 117
    objectives in, 91
Open approach, to evaluations, 137
Open content, 103–104, 109–110
Organizational context, 62–65
Outcome-based education, 26
Outdoor education, 175
Out-of-class work, 124–125
Outside work, 124–125

P
Panel discussions, 119
Pass-fail grades, 155
Patterns, of learning, 33
PBL (problem-based learning), 28
Pedagogy of the Oppressed (Freire), 52
Peer tutoring, 55–56
Perceptions, of learning, 142
Peripheral participation, 27
Philosophy, educational, 11–12, 86
Physical context, 69–71
Pirsig, R. M., 101

If you enjoyed this book, you may also like these:

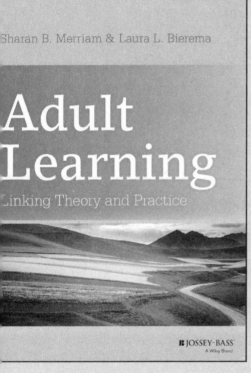

Want to connect?

Like us on Facebook
http://www.facebook.com/JBHigherEd

Subscribe to our newsletter
www.josseybass.com/go/higheredemail

Follow us on Twitter
http://twitter.com/JBHigherEd

Go to our Website
www.josseybass.com/highereducation

Department of
Adult & Community Education